Blowing
the
Whistle

Blowing
the
Whistle

Paul van Buitenen

Politico's
PUBLISHING

First published in Great Britain 2000
Published by Politico's Publishing
8 Artillery Row
Westminster
London
SW1P 1RZ

Tel 020 7931 0090
Fax 020 7828 8111
Email publishing@politicos.co.uk
Website www.politicos.co.uk/publishing

A catalogue record of this book is available from the British Library.

ISBN 1902301463

Translated by Lorna Dale
Printed and bound in Great Britain by St. Edmundsbury Press.
Cover Design by Advantage

First Published in the Netherlands 1999
by Ten Have
Julianalaan 11
Baarn
Postbus 133
3740 AC Baarn
Netherlands

CONTENTS

January 2000

On 9 December 1998, in my position as assistant-auditor in the Commission's Financial Control Directorate, I blew the whistle on the Commission's poor management of the fight against internal irregularities and fraud. I forwarded an incriminating 34 page letter, including almost 600 pages of reference material, to a Member of the European Parliament. This was the acceleration of an ongoing series of events that finally led to the resignation of the entire Commission little more than three months later.

On 15 March 1999 the first report of the Committee of Independent experts was published. Support for the Commission within the European Parliament evaporated immediately. This Committee of five "wise persons" was called in by the European Parliament to investigate my allegations and it largely confirmed what I had been saying all along. More important even than that was the report's devastating conclusion that it was not easy to find anyone in the Commission with a proper sense of responsibility.

As a result of this, I was suspended for 4 months on half pay. I was reinstated in April, but banned from further auditing tasks and was finally disciplined with a reprimand that was severe in its wording. I have considered leaving the Commission's services as I doubted whether there would still be a basis for me to continue my efforts to help improve the organisation from within. However, quite unexpectedly the previously anonymous support from many colleagues materialised in more visible form through my election as a staff representative with a high number of preferential votes. I decided to stay on board.

The Committee of Independent Experts issued their final report on 10 September 1999. It presented detailed recommendations for a thorough administrative reform of the Commission. This final report has been acknowledged by the European Parliament as a very good basis for reform.

The new Commission under President Prodi also promised grass root reforms. As a result, a Consultative document on the envisaged Commission reform was been proposed by Commissioner Neil Kinnock to the Commission staff on 18 January 2000. As elected staff representative and prominent member of my staff union "Renouveau et Démocratie", I hope to be in a position to work on a real reform of the European Commission.

My book was first published in the Netherlands (*Strijd voor Europa*, Ten Have) and Germany (*Unbestechlich fur Europa*, Brunnen Verlag) in the autumn of 1999. In this English edition I am pleased to include an extra chapter at the end, which brings the situation up to date.

Paul van Buitenen

Brussels, February 2000

INTRODUCTION

Europe Deserves Better

'It is with deep regret that I write this letter to you'. That was how I began my report on fraud and irregularities in the European Commission. It was my last resort after I had seen my criticisms swept under the table for the past year. It caused a major stir. The papers were full of sensational headlines about the people involved, but I was glad to see that they also exposed the root of the problem, *De Morgen*, for instance, published the story under the headline 'European Commission sabotages its own internal audit department'. That was what I had been trying to achieve.

Breach of Confidentiality

In the report I described how I had tried unsuccessfully to put a stop to corruption, irregularities and fraud in the European Commission through the proper channels, by using internal procedures. As a European official I was bound by the regulations which prohibited me from reporting problems of that nature to the Parliament. An official can only be released from the duty of confidentiality by the Commission—which is a problem when it is the Commission itself that is implicated.

Low Election Turnout

In my relatively brief career in the European Commission, I came across more and more examples where things did not look quite right—and unfortunately this was borne out on closer inspection. But the Commission's internal auditors seemed unable or unwilling to take any action. Malpractice was allowed to continue, threatening the credibility and the future of the Commission and the European Union as a whole. This was clearly demonstrated by the low turnout in the last European elections. The electorate and the campaigners were not to blame. It was because of the corruption.

More Transparent Structures

I firmly believe that the future lies in real cooperation within Europe, but the organisations involved in that cooperation need to be more accountable and transparent. In order to make a constructive contribution to the public interest I was eventually forced to breach confidentiality and report the problems to an outside but undeniably legitimate control body, the European Parliament. At the press conference on 9 December the Greens made the report public.

Heads to Roll?

The report was a bombshell and in the end it placed a bomb under the Commission as well. But it was never my intention to bring down the Commission. It has only itself to thank for that. I would have much preferred simply to get on with my work as a European Official and not be fobbed off when I came across irregularities. The same goes for many of my colleagues. In the past they have had to suffer in silence time and time again when they uncover irregularities and nothing is done. Sometimes pressure has even been put on them to withdraw their investigation reports. A number of my colleagues helped me when I became so disgusted at what was going on that I decided to start doing some detective work. The end result was the report – and now this book. In fact they also put themselves at risk by supplying me with information that would otherwise have remained hidden.

Whistle Blowing Has its Price

It has undoubtedly been regarded until now as worse than a crime for a European official to breach confidentiality. My action has had drastic consequences for myself and my family as well as for the European Commission. I was suspended for a month on half pay and then moved to another job. Disciplinary proceedings against me are still ongoing and the outcome is still undecided at the time of writing. When this book was published I and my family faced an uncertain future. As the person exposing the corruption I have so far suffered far more than the officials and commissioners who were probably or demonstrably mixed up in it. A whistleblower has no protection in Europe—in fact quite the reverse.

At the same time my wife and I have certainly been given a good deal of moral support from other quarters over the past year. I have had a heartening response from the public and strong backing from the smaller political groups in the European Parliament especially the Greens and religious groups.

A System out of Control

In this book I describe the serious deficiencies that colleagues and I found in the way the Commission is run. I am not trying to settle any scores. My main aim is to show how easily people can become involved in or connive at irregularities, fraud and corruption. The lack of proper control and management undermines the whole system. The Commission urgently needs cleaning up. The relatively small number of senior officials guilty of malpractice are tarnishing the Commission's image. For years they have managed to escape prosecution. That has to change with the new Commission under President Prodi. I hope that this book will help to achieve that.

How the Book is Set Out

The first chapter contains a short critical outline of the European structures mentioned further on in the book. I go on to explain how I myself worked within these structures and how I saw the European Union's good intentions defeated in various ways. I describe my own experiences and my dilemma as a Christian in going against the authorities. Did I really do the right thing? A few notorious examples of fraud are summarised under different subject headings. Each chapter begins with a brief explanation of the organisation and aims of the European programme and an introduction to the main players. The final chapters describe the repercussions of the report's publication for me and my family, the media hype, the suspension, the disciplinary proceedings and the uncertain future, I am grateful to my wife Edith for allowing me to use short extracts from her diary which show how the whole episode has affected her and the rest of our family,

CHAPTER ONE

Europe in a Nutshell

The original Dutch edition of this book was called *Fighting for Europe* because I firmly believe that the future for all of us lies in European cooperation. But that does not mean that we should be moving towards a United States of Europe.

The world is becoming smaller all the time and many problems can no longer be solved at national level. Measures such as improvements in working hours, better animal transport conditions, the ban on child labour and restrictions on the emission of harmful gases affect competition. If one European country allows the transport of animals for days on end, working days of more than eight hours, child labour and the unrestricted emission of harmful gases whereas another does not, firms in the first country are going to be able to produce more cheaply. If we want to take measures like that without distorting competition in the European market, it is better that they should be taken at the European level.

A lot of good work done in the European Commission is inspired by good intentions of this kind. It is not all corruption and malpractice. Fortunately real corruption is the exception and fraud is by no means an everyday occurrence. Most of the work is done as it should be, with worthwhile programmes making a genuine contribution to Europe's future. This book will unfortunately come as a revelation to many of my colleagues who have put in years of hard and conscientious work at the Commission.

★ ★ ★

HOW THE EUROPEAN UNION WORKS

A Parliament with Limited Powers

As citizens of Europe we elect a European Parliament every five years. This democratically elected body only has a limited power of decision. In fact the real power still lies with the national governments. The important decisions are taken by the Council of Ministers, the European Union's highest authority. The Council of Ministers is made up of ministers from the Member States and in that sense represents all the national governments. However the national parliaments have no democratic control over the Council's decisions. This is referred to as Europe's 'democratic deficit' and it has to be made up by the European Parliament if there is to be proper democracy in Europe.

It is true that the European Parliament is gradually acquiring more decision-making powers. Its most important right is the right to vote on the budget and Parliament uses this to consolidate its influence in other areas.

Since, generally speaking, the Parliament has no power of decision, its role is purely advisory. If the Commission is proposing to take a decision that the MEPs do not like, the Parliament has to try to head it off by refusing to allocate funds or allocating only a limited amount. The right to vote on the budget is such a powerful instrument that Parliament often uses it just to have some say in the matter.

Unanswered Questions

But because the elected European Parliament has so few powers it does not even exercise its democratic control function effectively. It has often surprised me that the Commission does not answer quite pertinent questions from MEPs who are clearly well-briefed on the subject, or if it answers them at all it takes six months to do so. Not only is Parliament allowed to ask questions, it has a duty to force the Commission to answer them if necessary.

I hope to see the Commission and Parliament operating more democratically in future. In any event the Commission can no longer get away with simply ignoring an MEP or group of MEPs when they are looking for an answer. From now on this can have repercussions.

The Commission and the Right of Initiative

Although it is the Council of Ministers that takes the decisions, it would be virtually impossible for ministers to be responsible for everything that happens in Europe as well as in their national ministries. That is where the European Commissioners come in. There are 20 Commissioners, nominated by the national governments. The larger Member States have two each, the smaller States one. The Commissioners do not take major supranational decisions on European Union policies but they do decide on the planning and implementation of those policies. This planning function is known as the European Commission's right of initiative. Decisions are taken by the Council of Ministers and—particularly when funds have to be allocated for European programmes—by the European Parliament.

Europe Comes First

The Commissioners operate like a council of ministers. They must be apolitical and always act in the interests of the European Union. Commissioners should never protect their own national interests.

Commissioners are in charge of DGs (Directorates-General), official bodies similar to our national ministries.

The Commissioners are responsible for the running of the Commission as a whole and can be challenged on this. They are jointly responsible for all major planning decisions, in any field. They therefore have to be aware of what the other Commissioners are doing. Important decisions and discussions must be communal. This system is deliberately designed to safeguard Commissioners against national influence.

People Who Live in Glasshouses

After my report was published some of the Commissioners repeatedly claimed in front of the cameras that they had done nothing wrong and they were being penalised because a few of their colleagues had been guilty of abuses and misconduct. In view of the way the Commission operates, that is a misrepresentation. It is inconceivable that if they were working as they should be they would have failed to notice over a period of four years that some of their fellow Commissioners were consistently behaving in a completely unacceptable manner. For years they had had enough indications for them to intervene or have an investigation set up. But apart from, for instance, writing a letter to say that something was wrong, they did nothing to put a stop to this malpractice and in the end they paid for it.

European Programmes

The Commissioners' right of initiative means that the Commission can develop programmes to improve cooperation in Europe in all kinds of areas, for example programmes to promote cooperation in science and education, employment in less-favoured regions and so on.

European projects normally have to involve at least three or four Member States. Projects also have to meet various other criteria, depending on the nature of the programme. In some cases non-profitmaking organisations such as universities are called upon to participate. Sometimes particular regions have to work together and sometimes the programmes are designed to improve the status of minority languages or groups suffering discrimination (gypsies, the handicapped, the unemployed, immigrants).

Cabinets: Necessary but not Transparent

European Commissioners each have their own cabinet, which is quite separate from the official organisation, the DGs. This is a staff of personal advisers who can be appointed outside the Commission's normal recruitment procedures. Unlike a national minister who is only responsible for his own field of policy a European Commissioner has a far wider range of subjects to cover. So there is something to be said for their having a small circle of close colleagues and confidantes to make sure that the Commissioner is properly briefed.

Conflicts of Interest

The staff of the Commissioners' cabinets are on the whole competent people who are a useful complement to the work of the Commission. But there are cases where cabinets employ friends or even relatives of the Commissioner. In my view even apparent conflicts of interests must be avoided. With work of this kind, where democratic government and its implementation are so closely linked, it is undesirable for partners or relatives to be given paid jobs. However I have repeatedly come across these situations at all levels in the European institutions, as I will explain later on in this book.

Some of the Commissioners had very large private staffs and furthermore it was not clear who was paying these special advisers. I hope that this will change under the new Commission. From now on the rule that no Commissioner may have more than six people in his cabinet is to be very strictly applied. The traditional arrangement where everyone in the cabinet—except one, for the sake of appearances—is the same nationality as the Commissioner also needs to go. Mr Prodi has already set a precedent by appointing an Irishman as his chef de cabinet rather than an Italian.

Lobbying in Brussels

Lobbying is common in Europe. There is nothing wrong with lobbying as such. It is quite legitimate for a citizen or someone acting on his behalf to bring his interests to the attention of the European institutions. If a car manufacturer finds that new European directives might be detrimental to his interests he can, for instance, employ a lobbying firm in Brussels to draw this to the attention of MEPs and the Commission in official letters. 'It is all very well for you to set emission standards which cars have to meet, but I am selling fewer and fewer cars because they are becoming too expensive and in the long run that is costing us jobs'.

Lobbying therefore has to be open and above board, so that it can be controlled. Lobbying becomes underhand if an MEP on a committee that delivers opinions on the emission of waste gases is found to be on the payroll of a motor manufacturer, or if an MEP called upon to give an opinion on the European IT market turns out to be in the pay of a computer company. To many this is a self-evident truth but others prefer to ignore it.

Streamlined Organisation

The European Commission has only a small number of officials. People might laugh at that and say there are too many, but in fact the Commission employs fewer people than, for instance, the cities of London or Paris. Commission staff work in Directorates-General, abbreviated to DGs.

To avoid employing too many staff and doing more work in-house than is strictly necessary, the Commission uses outside offices to run its programmes. In practice the staff of these offices work entirely or partially for a DG. With the addition of countless consultants, national experts and temporary staff recruited for short-term jobs, clearly there are many different categories of staff working in the European institutions. The DGs for instance have various kinds of staff and it is not at all clear whether they are being paid by the Commission, a Member State or an office which in turn is being paid by the Commission.

TAOs: Powerful Contractors

Technical Assistance Offices, or TAOs, are very important in Brussels. After the Commission has formulated a European programme it has to be implemented. The policy guidelines and priorities for the programme are established, along with the budgets. Often officials in the DGs (and hence the Commission) have no further involvement in the practical administration of the programme. The work is contracted out to a TAO.

This is done through an open invitation to tender. A call for tenders is published in the Official Journal, announcing the programme and inviting interested parties to tender for its management. They are allowed a certain period to apply for information on the programme, study it and submit a proposal. Of the hundreds of people and organisations requesting information, only a few dozen eventually submit a serious proposal.

All the tenders are processed in the DG concerned and finally a selection committee makes its choice. This is based amongst other things on price, the organisation's experience with other projects and the guarantees of continuity the organisation is able to offer, for instance contingency measures for staff sickness or when the programme has to be extended to include new member states joining the EU. Thus the Commission buys in some of the administrative machinery to run the programme. The offices are not supposed to involve themselves in politics. The TAO is of course required to submit regular interim reports on how the programme is progressing.

The TAO in turn manages the projects allocated to other contractors, who implement the projects financed under the programme. This is also done through a European tendering procedure, with a selection committee ultimately awarding the contract to the organisations with the best proposals. The TAO responsible for managing the European programme can often delegate staff to the project selection committee.

A Small Circle

Consequently the Commission only has a limited number of permanent staff. But ultimately the TAO structure clearly operates as a privatised bureaucracy. Some specialist organisations work regularly if not exclusively for the European Commission, albeit for different DGs. Offices of this kind can only survive if they always have a full order book. That means that a number of people in the office need to have a good relationship with Commission officials who can influence the selection committee's decision. Another way of ensuring regular orders from the Commission (and thus regular income) is to have a member of staff or department in one of these consultancy offices working full-time on the submission of tenders and plans for European tenders.

The problem here is that, whilst it is an advantage to use a known office with specialist skills because this provides reasonable guarantees that the European programme will be properly run, the administration work for the Commission is done mostly within existing networks. New and untried organisations have no chance of breaking into the field. In a fair tendering procedure the selection committee might well not choose the very best candidate from the hundred or two hundred applicants, but a selection committee with a little bit of experience will certainly pick a good contractor. In practice, however, the Commission all too often falls back on old favourites and European Commission programmes are run by a select band of regular contractors or groups of contractors with European subsidies as their sole source of revenue.

These are the less desirable consequences of the tender system, even when the rules are properly applied. Irregularities only occur when contracts are awarded to a contractor time after time and other parties have no opportunity to compete or submit a tender. Even this is still possible within the rules. The larger the project, the stricter the tender procedure has to be. The procedure for smaller projects is more flexible. If the cost of a project is below a certain level it is possible simply to place the order. So if a European official wants to use a particular contractor a project can be split into several small jobs falling under the limit, with more than one quotation.

I have actually seen a contractor's tender being written within the department. Obviously that is quite unacceptable. It is also wrong that a contractor should be able to submit an identical project proposal three or four years in succession.

In the Leonardo da Vinci affair—which I shall discuss in more detail in Chapter 4—a TAO was even set up for the express purpose of running a European programme. The TAO was not a separate department of a large existing consultancy, but a firm set up solely to act as the TAO for the Leonardo da Vinci programme. That meant that the firm was entirely dependent on the subsidy. To me that is really not on.

Some organisations are tipped off by the Commission well in advance that a particular European programme is being developed. Sometimes people cleverly take advantage of this. An interest group makes sure that at around the time the European tender is due a technical assistance office is ready and fully prepared. This is still just about within the limits of what is permissible. In the case of Leonardo it even turned out to have been a subsidiary of the interest group, in which all the shareholders were of the same nationality. Later one more shareholder was added, who happened to be of the same nationality as the Commissioner responsible.

Once the contract has been awarded the TAO becomes a powerful organisation in the Commission, at least as far as the running of that particular programme is concerned. The TAO has plenty of work to contract out and has to liaise regularly on the work with European officials in the DG. This provides an opportunity to wangle some extra funds, which can be used for instance to make interim payments to advisers.

Thus the TAO system, which was designed to streamline the administrative machinery, not only defeats that object but also creates a specific risk of irregularities. These are not just idle rumours. I have come across such cases myself in my time at the Commission, which I shall explain in more detail later.

No Teeth: The Fraud Prevention Unit

Clearly every system has its weaknesses. That is why effective control mechanisms are important, to ensure that everything is done by the book and to make any changes that are necessary.

The unwritten rule that everything has to be handled within the institution and nothing must be disclosed means that the Commission's control mechanisms are not working. In the world of politics people are reluctant to go to law. Problems are dealt with internally. Criminal proceedings are not generally brought against corrupt officials or people who commit forgery (which is a criminal offence). Criminal proceedings indirectly bring everything out into the open. Even internal disciplinary proceedings are often not instituted because they can quickly leak out. The Commission is then faced with the choice of starting disciplinary proceedings to really get to the bottom of the problem or trying to resolve the matter internally, for instance by transferring the official to an innocuous job where he is no longer handling budgets. People escape punishment and these practices can easily proliferate. There is an obligation to keep things quiet.

This caginess is supposed to prevent the Commission and the European Union being seen in a bad light. But in the long run it is actually more damaging than transparency and openness.

Culture also plays a part. In my experience it is not really a question of the difference between Northern and Southern European cultures. I have come across a serious case of fraud by a senior official from Northern Europe and highly conscientious and trustworthy officials from the South. It is certainly true that with some nationalities the Commissioners and officials prefer to work closely with their compatriots or people speaking the same language. That is understandable, because it makes communication easier, but it can easily lead to favouritism and bias. There is more scope for this in some cultures than in others.

What is Fraud?
In the European Commission—at least according to the routine

practice of the internal fraud prevention unit—only corruption on the part of a European official (in other words the acceptance of goods or services, for instance from a contractor as 'kickback payments') can be termed fraud. Apart from this narrow definition the Commission's fraud prevention unit, until recently known as UCLAF, imposes other restrictions. For instance it will only open an investigation if it is provided with incontrovertible proof. Obviously it would not be practicable for the department to start investigating every rumour or piece of gossip. But even when there are consistent indications of irregularity it does not institute an investigation until there is already exhaustive proof, whereas the department should actually initiate the investigation itself and get at the truth. In practice, however, it acts as a filter to the outside world.

In my view the fraud prevention unit should investigate other forms of fraud as well as corruption, for instance forgery, nepotism and other irregularities.

Things that are not really right but are not so serious as to be criminal offences, for instance a rigged tender procedure, are irregularities. I believe that it is the job of the fraud prevention unit to expose these, to ensure that they do not happen again and prevent more serious lapses.

But the unit's caution is understandable, because if it does not produce hard evidence of fraud—full-scale corruption with kickback payments according to its definition—the Commission does not consider it necessary to take the case to court (which is after all virtually the same as bringing it out in the open). That is why the department covers itself and requires proof before it will take any action.

Scarce Resources

Apart from that the fraud prevention unit has limited powers and very scarce resources. Often it cannot obtain any hard evidence because it comes up against a wall of silence. People are worried about their own jobs—which, in the light of my own experiences, I can fully appreciate—and the fraud prevention people have to be circumspect when they write up their findings. As a result anyone reading the report might easily conclude that everything is fine.

UCLAF needs people who can go through the accounts with a fine tooth comb. A lot of its staff are former police and customs officers and it has only a few people with legal experience and proper accountancy training who can pinpoint any problems. What Financial Control and the fraud prevention unit need, for example, is a section or even just one member of staff working full-time on comparing databases. Which names appear where? Which bank account numbers go with which names? Which people and organisations have the same address? This would bring to light any links; for instance an office working for various DGs (not that there is necessarily anything wrong in that). When evaluating a tender an official might for example ask for references to make certain that a contractor can carry out his project. UCLAF has recently been reorganised into the independent body OLAF. It remains to be seem whether this will resolve the problems I have outlined above.

Transparency and Openness

In the end openness is still, in my experience, the best method of control and sanction. This control has been exercised by the small groups in the European Parliament and the press. In response to that pressure a Committee of Wise Men was set up to investigate the situation and they came to a damning conclusion on the cover-ups in Brussels. In the past few months in particular I have had reason to be grateful to the press.

Because, whilst a new Commission has now been appointed and the disciplinary proceedings against me are still continuing (in fact their scope is even being widened), the European Union is back to business as usual and the people in Parliament who spoke up on my behalf are in danger of falling silent.

CHAPTER TWO

The Brussels Maze

I am an accountant by profession. I studied for the chartered accountancy exams at evening classes for six years, but had to give up because I found them too difficult to combine with a young family. I got a job as a budget planner in the library at Delft Technical University and moved with my family to Rotterdam. We had a nice subsidised house which we owned, I was in a job which I enjoyed and I got on well with my boss.

Leafing through the *Algemeen Dagblad* one day, I noticed a curious advertisement with a picture of flags in a semi-circle. The European Commission in Brussels was recruiting for a reserve list of administrative assistants at the European Commission and the European Court of Auditors. I knew very little about the European institutions, but it aroused my curiosity and I showed the advert to my wife Edith. At first she was concerned and surprised. 'What are you doing looking at job ads?' she said. 'You have a good job at the university and that was why we moved to Rotterdam'.

'I'm not looking at job ads in general', I said. 'I'm just curious. Anyway it looks as if it might take a long time and I probably don't meet the criteria. And I can always say no'.

Eventually Edith agreed that I should write to Brussels.

Lobbying for an Application

Months went by and we heard nothing. Our lives went on as

usual. After a while I was invited to take a series of tests. Again months went by before we heard the results. As I got more into the selection procedure I started reading up on the European institutions. There is a lot that is not widely known and it proved to be more interesting than I had thought. A friend of ours who was fluent in French began helping me to learn French.

At the beginning of 1989 I suddenly received a letter of congratulation telling me I had been put on the list of successful candidates. I would be called for an interview. It was difficult to choose between my job in Delft and the Brussels job and I kept putting off the decision. As it turned out I did not have to decide anything for a while because the promised invitation to Brussels did not materialise.

I had certainly realised by then that I would earn a lot of money in Brussels. A career in Brussels was a real opportunity for someone like myself without a degree.

I rang the Foreign Ministry in The Hague and a couple of Dutch officials in Brussels to find out more about the opportunities and how the procedure worked. Applying for a job with the European Commission was very different from applying for a job in the Netherlands. As a 'successful candidate' I was on a list but that did not mean I would actually be accepted. The list was a pool from which candidates were selected to fill a vacant post if no one was found inside the European institutions. So if you wanted to get into the European institutions you could not always go straight into the job you were most interested in. If I wanted to be considered for an interview I had to draw attention to myself, because after a while the list of candidates would be out of date and would have to be updated. In short, I had to go and lobby for myself if I wanted at least to be invited for an interview. The very word lobbying put me off.

I thought it over and talked to Edith. If I really wanted to pursue this it was the only way. It was already a year and a half since I had started. So eventually I decided to go along with the whole rigmarole. I sent my CV to everyone in the Commission who was prepared to have a look at it. I wrote to all 23 of the Commission's Directorates-General, the European Statistical Office, the Court of Auditors and so on. Letters by ordinary post, letters by recorded delivery, letters by courier. With the help of a contact one of these many letters finally ended up in the right office.

During this long period I had also got involved in another European Commission procedure, this time for temporary officials. The procedure was a bit shorter and there was only an oral test. I passed it and was called to the personnel office in Brussels. When I asked if I should accept the temporary job or whether I would do better to wait and see if I was offered a permanent post, the answer was vague. In a temporary job I would start on a higher scale. But because I was on the waiting list for permanent posts it would be easier for me to transfer to a permanent post at the same higher level. I was told that this would put me nearly ten years ahead in my career. I thought this was a bit odd and I did not entirely believe it. I decided not to take the temporary job.

Nearly two years after first answering the advert I was invited for an interview. It was for a job in the contract unit in DG XII, the DG for science and research.

I later heard that about 16,000 people from all over Europe had replied to the advert. Only about a hundred of them would eventually be taken on by the Commission.

At the interview I met the German head of unit, a friendly, slightly older man, and the British head of section. They seemed well-disposed towards me at the interview. It was apparently in my favour that I worked at a university. They managed a lot of contracts with universities. They asked if I would like a job in the contract unit. I was extremely relieved and of course I said yes straightaway. Then I realised to my astonishment that they were worried that I might still go to another department. They explained to me that I would have to come to Brussels for a medical. Other departments often used that as an opportunity to invite you for an interview so that they did not have to pay the travel expenses. Often candidates found better jobs and quickly switched to another department. I told them I was not like that and if I gave my word that was it, even if I were to be offered better jobs afterwards. In fact I did have to turn down other invitations later on.

I waited months. Expenditure had been frozen and it was not certain when I would be able to take up the post. Apparently this was a general problem throughout the Commission.

Finally, on 1 February 1990, I started my job as a European official in Brussels. I was put in the B grade, for people with a good secondary education. A grade officials have completed a four-year vocational qualification or university degree. C grade officials provide support services such as administrative and secretarial work.

After the long and arduous selection and application procedure I felt I had been specially chosen and I was highly motivated when I started the job. I was really proud when I got my European number plates for my car. I felt like a real European!

Edith: 'Paul and I went house-hunting in Overijse, close to Brussels. A colleague had told us there was a house for sale near where he lived and he said it was not at all expensive considering the house prices on the outskirts of Brussels. We arranged to go and see it. But as we were following the owner around the house Paul and I kept looking at each other in disbelief. Surely we would never be able to pay for such a lovely detached house! But with Paul's new salary we could actually afford it. We stopped on the way back to let it sink in. After all those years in a subsidised house in a terrace, we were now going to live in a detached house with a beautiful garden. We couldn't believe it. It was too good to be true'.

Politics and Real Life

The first few weeks were very hard. French seemed to be the main working language. The first departmental meetings I went to were all in French and I had trouble following what was going on. Later I asked a Flemish colleague what the word 'gestionnaire' meant. I had heard it a lot and I really needed to know.

'That's what you are, Paul', she said. I didn't understand.

The contract unit had a staff of about 50, of various nationalities, some permanent and some temporary. About 20 of them were budget managers or 'gestionnaires' like me. Each of us managed between 200 and 400 research contracts. Part of my job was to deal with scientific cooperation contracts with Israel. This cooperation was – to be a bit irreverent – rather like Israel being in the Eurovision Song Contest. Strictly speaking Israel was not a European country, but it did participate in European programmes, including a few scientific research projects, under certain conditions. My job was to arrange new contracts and make payments under existing contracts.

As a motivated and committed official I read everything that I came across in the papers about Europe. Of course I also followed the political debates in the European Parliament. In 1990 the European Parliament still had very limited powers. The only real power it had was the right to vote on the budget. That meant that Parliament could approve the Commission's budgets beforehand and subsequently agree the Commission's expenditure. At one point the European Parliament used that right to freeze expenditure on cooperation with Israel because of Israel's policy in the occupied territories.

As soon as I saw that I spoke to my head of section. Did Parliament's decision mean that I had to suspend the contract proposals and current payments for Israel?

At first he looked at me in amazement and asked what gave me that idea. I told him what I had been reading. Patiently he explained to me that I obviously didn't understand that the political decisions taken in the European Parliament had very little to do with the Commission's day-to-day business.

It was also part of my job to go out and call on contractors and check that the final accounts were correct. We carried out these audits for large projects or when there were several projects close together, or if it seemed that there might be problems with a project. But I quickly realised that it was largely up to us where we went. One colleague, for instance, only went to audit projects if there was a golf course nearby.

No Smoke Without Fire?

In any organisation or community where people work together there is gossip and rumour and innocent chat over drinks. In that respect Brussels is no different from other places, whether they be commercial firms, universities, ministries or even villages. What did strike me, though, was that rumours and gossip about irregularities cropped up far more often than in my previous jobs.

For instance a colleague in the personnel department told me a remarkable story about a Mr François, who had been appointed to the Court of Auditors. As a former Director-General he got a generous pension from the Commission. At the Court of

Auditors he was now being paid almost the same salary as a European Commissioner (nearly £6,000 a month net of tax). Under the rules his new salary obviously had to be offset against the pension, which meant that the whole of the pension would have to be stopped. But according to the rumours he was absolutely determined to draw both salaries and, despite objections from DG IX (Personnel) and DG XX (Financial Control), he had managed to wangle it. The Commission President, Jacques Delors, was said to have intervened personally in his favour. It was a tall story and I didn't really know whether or not to believe it.

Years later, on an official trip abroad, it came up again. In the bar at the hotel it suddenly came back to me. 'Hey, Erhardt, do you know that story?' I outlined it briefly. I asked my colleague if he happened to know anything about it.

'Yes, it's true,' said Erhardt. 'From what I heard Jacques Delors' cabinet even put pressure on the Director-General of Financial Control at one point to withdraw his objections and let it go through. I don't know exactly what happened, but there was definitely something funny going on'.

Later on, after Mr François had died, his widow had apparently insisted she should carry on getting a higher pension. It was not clear to me whether DG IX put a stop to this, but it did show that there was at least some truth in the earlier story of his being paid twice.

To Social Affairs

In 1992 DG XII was reorganised and all the 'gestionnaires' were decentralised. Preferring to decide for myself where I was going, I transferred to DG V, the Directorate-General responsible for social affairs. As the only contract manager, I began working for the employment policy unit. The unit dealt with European employment market statistics and analyses. The internal application procedure was pleasant and informal, which I liked. I was hoping to become the financial right-hand man for my head of unit, Mr Jenkins.

Shortly after I started the unit held a get-together and I met colleagues and other staff from the unit. After a while a man came up to me. He didn't say who he was but asked me straight out how I was getting on in Jenkins' department. I was a bit surprised and embarrassed because I thought that by then I knew all my colleagues in the unit quite well. He obviously knew me. So after some hesitation I asked him who he was.

He looked at me and said, 'You're the new contract person in this department, aren't you?'

I nodded, a bit reluctantly.

'Well,' he went on 'you'll know soon enough who I am. I am very important to this unit and you'll be dealing with a lot of work from me. Anyhow, good luck with the new job.'

He walked off with his glass in his hand to join another group. A little riled, I asked one of my colleagues who the man was. Did I have to take any notice of him and if so how and why?

My colleague told me the man was called Gary Fasting and he was British like our boss. He wasn't a Eurocrat but one of the regular outside contractors that our boss Mr Jenkins liked doing business with. I was taken aback that an outside contractor should behave so arrogantly in his client's office.

In fact Fasting seemed to be in and out of our office a lot. Another day I came across Jenkins and Gary Fasting in Jenkins' office. They were drinking whisky and laughing about some stories going around the Brussels grapevine. Fasting was laughing and saying that some of the illustrations for his report on the employment situation in Europe came from his small son's geography atlas. That irked me when I knew that the Commission had paid more than £635,000 a year for Fasting's organisation to prepare the report.

Employment has been one of the most important political issues since the 1980s and a lot of hard work has been devoted to it, in Europe as well as nationally. Since the mass unemployment of the early '80s, whole sections of society have grown up in every country in Western Europe, which are unlikely ever to get a job or any work experience or earn any money at all. A range of European programmes has been set up over the years for employment schemes, in large towns and backward regions and for groups in danger of being overlooked, such as young people and the long-term unemployed. DG V was one of the Directorates-General running these programmes.

One morning my colleague Claude Olivier came into my room in great excitement. 'Did you see the programme with Jacques Delors on French television last night?'

I looked up with interest. 'No, what was it about?'

Claude told me that Jacques Delors was live in the studio, answering questions from a studio audience. At one point a man stood up in the audience and produced two copies of our unit's reports on employment in the European Community. He explained to Delors that the reports were for different years five years apart, probably 1987 and 1992. He then read a passage from each report. It was soon clear, to the audience's amusement, that the two passages on the current situation were absolutely identical. The man confronted Delors with this and asked him how it was possible. 'What is the Commission actually doing with the taxpayers' money?'

Delors was clearly embarrassed and said he would have it looked into.

Claude was full of indignation. 'Now it's finally going to come out that Gary Fasting just throws something together and for that we pay more than £600,000 a year!'

Unfortunately that was the last I heard of it. Apparently Delors never took Jenkins to task over it.

The Disappearing Laptop

When I began working in social affairs I started finding out what could be done with budgets in Brussels. At one point I received the final invoice for a relatively small project that one of my predecessors had dealt with. I got the file out and looked through it quickly. I noticed straightaway that the final invoice was identical to the budget submitted previously. To an auditor this can be an indication that the invoice is just a way of getting the final balance paid and bears no relation to actual expenditure. I raised my eyebrows and had a closer look at the file.

One of the items of expenditure was a laptop computer. That was a bit odd; do you need to buy a new computer specially for a small project? When I checked I saw that the computer had also been shown in the budget previously. So that was correct. I looked to see if the computer had been properly written off and then I noticed something else. Normally a computer is an investment that you write off over at least three years. With such a small project the computer could obviously be used for another project afterwards.

I decided to ring the contractor. I got through after a couple of attempts. I asked why the computer had been charged to the project in full. The person I was speaking to was surprised. 'But wasn't that what we agreed?'

I replied that I had actually seen that part of the purchase price of the computer was already included in the budget

'Part? What do you mean? Who exactly are you? It was agreed the computer would be charged to the project in full, wasn't it?'

Now it was my turn to be surprised. I sensed that something

was not right. I explained that I was new to the unit and I didn't know exactly how things worked. But I had to make the final payment and I obviously wanted to find out first if I had understood the situation correctly.

I asked him to explain it to me again. The contractor told me that the laptop had been bought because the report had to be written on it.

It seemed odd to me that a report should have to be written on a laptop specially bought for the purpose. I also pointed out that of course only part of the cost of a new computer could be charged to the project.

'Only part? No, the whole computer. We bought the computer specially for this project, not for any others.'

I couldn't believe my ears and I said so on the phone. 'And what are you going to do with it now?'

The person on the other end of the line was laughing at my ignorance. I was obviously naïve. 'You have the computer!'

'What?' I exclaimed. 'We have the computer? How's that?'

It was then explained to me. The arrangement was that the contractors could work on the project if they were willing to allow in the project budget for the purchase of a computer, which would then be handed over to Jenkins' department. I was at a loss for words and put the phone down in bewilderment. I had to take this in. So where was the laptop? Who was using it?

I decided to ring my predecessor. He should know the details. I phoned him in his new department and asked how he was getting on. He had since been promoted and given a more responsible job. After a few more civilities I reminded him of the project and asked if he knew what had happened to the laptop.

There was silence on the other end of the line and then he told me he had it at home.

'But why have you got the computer at home?' I asked him.

My predecessor told me frostily that it was none of my business and that in any case it had been done with the permission of Mr Jenkins, the head of unit. I should ask him if I had any more questions. End of conversation.

Later I found that more PCs appeared to have come in via contractors and were on the Commission's inventory. These PCs were actually in the unit, together with a photocopier that officially was not on the inventory at all.

So project funds were regularly siphoned back to the department in one way or another via a contractor—sometimes in the form of equipment, but in some cases as staff. The Commission did not even know about some of the temporary staff around our department. They were employed through contractors by our head of unit, Mr Jenkins, and then worked in our unit at the Commission. I wondered if that was allowed and spoke to Mr Jenkins about it. However he came up with a strong argument, which I found it very difficult to counter. He pointed out that the Commission rules were much too strict for flexible budget management. In the long run the money was actually being used for the Commission; he was not lining his own pocket. He did have a point.

I didn't want to fall out with my new boss at this early stage and so I did not pursue it. But I had my own views about it. The more complex and the less transparent these arrangements were, the more difficult it was to keep a check on them. And the more difficult it is to keep a check on things, the more people are tempted to engage in a little 'creative accounting'. Where should the line be drawn?

Files Rejected

All the Commission's contract proposals and payments have to be systematically checked by Financial Control. Inevitably these checks were fairly superficial because of the enormous volume of work. Only when a file was picked out in a random check or, for instance, when the auditors had a tip-off, was it looked at very thoroughly.

When I had been with DGV for about six months I went to Financial Control with some of Jenkins' files. They were full of good plans, but none of them was exactly in line with the rules. The Financial Control department had sent the files back with critical comments. Actually I was quite pleased about this; other people felt the same way as I did. It was only my head of unit who thought differently.

In our unit the auditor, Iglesias, had the reputation of being difficult and inflexible. I had heard that he used to work for the court of auditors in Spain. Reluctantly I went to see him. Jenkins was expecting me to get the files passed, but I already knew that in view of the contents of the files and what I had heard of Iglesias this was going to be an impossible task. In any case it went against the grain.

I knocked on the door of his small office and asked if he had a minute to spare. He looked at me in amusement and gestured to me to sit down. We introduced ourselves. I didn't really know how to begin. My French was still not all that fluent and his was hard to understand because of his strong Spanish accent. Until then I had only spoken to him briefly on the phone. I started by explaining that we had taken note of his comments but that the Commission rules sometimes did not make enough allowances for the specific requirements of certain projects. Iglesias picked up the heap of files and leafed through them. He took one out and looked at me.

'You haven't been with Jenkins that long, have you? I think you came here with the right intentions, but I have to just explain a few things to you,' he began. 'Take this file, for example. This is typical of the sort of files I regularly get from Jenkins. The whole thing is full of holes and I know the contractor is one of Jenkins' regulars'.

I sat looking at him, speechless. 'We're at the end of the year,' Iglesias went on, 'There are still budgets to be worked out and there's not much time for auditing. Jenkins is an expert at putting files in at the last minute. He thinks they won't be looked at so carefully then and that's what he is waiting for.'

I looked at Iglesias in amazement. He was right. I had already heard the rumour from other colleagues in DG V. But I had not expected him to be so aware of the situation. There were in fact quite a few files in the pile for known contractors.

In principle several candidates had to be invited to tender when a contract was above a certain amount, in order to make a fair comparison and obtain a favourable price/quality ratio for the Commission. Only in special circumstances, for instance if time was very short, could a contractor be approached directly without a price comparison. These special circumstances seemed to occur quite often in Jenkins' case.

Iglesias and I talked for nearly two hours. By the end we had agreed on all the files. Iglesias had understood my position: obviously I had to go back to my boss with a result. At the same time he realised that I wanted to try and bring him better files in future. We arranged that I would leave certain files with him because they could be passed, but I had to take the worst ones back with me. I wasn't happy, but I had to admit that I came out of it well. I promised Iglesias that in future I would be much more critical of my boss's files. We shook hands and Iglesias said, 'That was a useful talk. I am glad we agree about what to do with the files'.

I told him I appreciated him being so understanding. I would speak to him first if there were any further problems.

As I walked back to my office I thought to myself that Iglesias wasn't really inflexible at all. He was a good financial controller and quite a few people could learn from his example. When I got back to Jenkins I put the remaining files on his desk. He came straight in and asked how the meeting had gone. 'Not as bad as I expected,' I began hesitantly. 'Iglesias made difficulties about a lot of the files ...'

Jenkins looked at me expectantly. 'But in the end quite a number were passed', I said hopefully. I was waiting for Jenkins to say he was not happy about that or even to sense that something was going on.

But to my amazement he was quite satisfied. He had not expected all the files to get through. Anything that did get past the auditors was evidently a bonus for him. However I said nothing to him about my frank discussion with Iglesias.

The Cancelled Trip

After I had been in Jenkins' department for about a year, I decided, after talking to Iglesias and the director's assistant Lieven Verstreepe, to go and audit one of Jenkins' main contractors in London. I was to go with Verstreepe and Iglesias might also be coming.

I told Jenkins that the trip was necessary because the contractor had received over 10% of the unit's total budget. Regular on-the-spot auditing was essential, otherwise it would not get past Financial Control. Jenkins didn't understand why Verstreepe needed to come too, but he couldn't see anything to object to in the plan and to my delight he authorised the trip.

I did not tell Jenkins at that stage that I had another reason for going to see the contractor in London. I wanted to look into kickback payments that Jenkins had set up with this contractor for extra staff. An official called Agnelli worked for his national government but was temporarily seconded to the Commission for an employment scheme in cooperation with the Eastern European countries. He was a good speaker and often went on official trips to explain Jenkins' Commission projects. As well as his national government salary he was entitled to a daily allowance from the Commission because he had various extra expenses. But things can move slowly in the Commission and this allowance took a long time to come through. Jenkins paid him an advance from one of his secret funds. In this case the money came from the contractor in London.

After a while the Commission paid Agnelli's allowance retroactively. But I was sure that Jenkins had not asked for his irregular extra payments back. So Agnelli was probably paid twice, with Jenkins' help.

I was perplexed as to why Jenkins had done that. What was the point? Maybe he had forgotten or there was some other - legitimate - reason. Or maybe the money had come back to the unit another way.

Shortly before we left I decided to tell Jenkins that I was planning to look into that in London. I warned him that if I uncovered any evidence that Agnelli had been paid twice I would do everything I could to get the money back.

The day before I was due to leave, when I already had my hotel booking and airline tickets, I was summoned to see Jenkins. He had decided to cancel my trip and withdraw his authorisation. I was furious, but I restrained myself. It was at that point I decided it was time to move on again.

Am I a Coward?

Thanks to a tip-off from Lieven Verstreepe I got a job in another unit in DGV, dealing with ECSC (European Coal and Steel Commission) aid. My new job was not particularly challenging but at least there were no irregularities in the department. My Flemish boss was very conscientious and had an encyclopaedic knowledge of ECSC regulations. I shared my office with a friendly Spaniard who did the same job as me. We got on well and had a lot of fun. In fact he even taught me in the office the hand clapping they do in flamenco!

I felt more relaxed there and could look back calmly at my previous unit. The more I looked at it from a distance, the more I realised that there was something wrong there. My conscience was bothering me. I had managed to find myself a secure position but my successor would be having to deal with the same problems. Was that really fair?

I was horrified at the mere thought of 'blowing the whistle', certainly from my new and secure position, but I was seriously considering whether to report Jenkins. I had a whole file on his wheeling and dealing, but I didn't really know what to do. Who should I ring? What auditing departments were there in the Commission? I made a list. Apart from Financial Control (DG XX), there was an internal auditing unit, IGS, and there was UCLAF, the fraud prevention unit. Verstreepe already knew what was going on and I asked his advice. He gave me the name and phone number of a colleague who worked in the right department.

I picked up the phone and dialled the number. With the receiver in my hand, I was suddenly afraid. Before anyone answered I put the receiver down. I just didn't dare to do it and I was worried about the repercussions. Jenkins would probably guess where the complaints had come from and that would be the end of my career in the Commission. It was much easier just to do nothing. Nobody would blame me for it. Surely it was not up to me to take unnecessary risks?

CHAPTER THREE

The Turning Point

The ball started rolling in any case. Almost a year later Michel Packard came to my room. We worked in the DG's finance section and he was a qualified accountant. He asked me if, as a former colleague of Jenkins', I still had access to documents pointing to irregularities in Jenkins' department. I feigned ignorance and asked what gave him that idea. Apparently Lieven Verstreepe had told him I had always been unhappy about what went on in the department. Packard explained that he had received complaints about Jenkins' activities from various different parties. The Director-General had asked him to collect evidence.

I was totally perplexed. Did that mean they were going to look into it after all, without me having to take any risks? I immediately decided to help them. I opened a drawer, rummaged around in my old papers and found the files I had tucked away. As I handed the pile over to Michel Packard it all came back to me what was in the documents. There were a number of contractors working from the same address and Jenkins signed contract after contract with them. One of the contractors had connections with his wife. And there was more.

Packard was obviously very pleased and took the files away with him. I was glad to be rid of the responsibility.

The Inspection

That year the head of my new unit announced that administrative procedures throughout DG V were to be reviewed.

Obviously we were curious to know why.

My boss said that it was just one of the routine inspections that took place periodically. It was to be carried out by Financial Control's Internal Audit section and involved random checks and interviews with officials. I turned out to be one of the officials they wanted to talk to. I was told that they were not interested in information about my present job but they wanted to speak to me about my work in Jenkins' department.

I was interviewed by two gentlemen from the Internal Audit. They put me at my ease with a few remarks about the weather and then explained the reasons for the inspection and my interview. All the managers were to be given a chance to express their views and a number of more junior officials in the financial administration—myself included—were being invited to interviews.

The meeting was mainly in the form of a questionnaire. I relaxed. Apparently they knew nothing about the irregularities in Jenkins' departments. They asked me about my job, my training, what my responsibilities were, how many documents I had to deal with and what procedures I followed. It was already some time since I had worked for Jenkins and I felt that I could not answer all the questions fully. Then the questions became broader. What had been my experiences in the department?

I plucked up courage and began to tell them. Not all the details, no contractors' names, but I did make it clear that there was a lot wrong with the system. I told them about the rigged tender procedures, my suspicions about Jenkins' conflicts of interest and so on.

At the end of the interview they told me that they

appreciated my attitude. In fact the chairman of the interviewing panel said that Financial Control needed people like me.

Some time later, when I was working in another Directorate-General, I heard that Jenkins had been sacked from his post. He had ended up working as an adviser and writing speeches. He would not be put in charge of a department again. This was presumably as a result of the enquiry into his activities. In the end he came out of it well. He was still a permanent official and had kept the same grade. That meant that he still got the same salary, over £4,500 a month net.

A Ray of Light

Financial management and control was certainly my forte, but I really wanted to do something a bit more challenging in the Commission. At home I was very involved in education through my children's schools and I had joined the parents' association.

Because of my interest, I applied in 1995 for a job in DG XXII, the Directorate-General for education, training and youth.

In one of the introductory discussions I made it clear that I did not want to have anything more to do with contract management. I was keen to be involved in challenging work in European programmes and I warned my future boss that they could not rely on my cooperation if I came across any irregularities. I had had enough of those in the past.

The head of unit was impressed with my attitude. 'We could certainly do with someone like you here!'

They needed someone in the unit who could keep a tight rein on budgets. But he assured me that all the contract management was done centrally and not in the units. I could work on the actual projects and develop my computer and Internet skills.

This move to DG XXII was a turning point for me. When I started in September 1995, little did I know what I would find there and what the consequences would be for me and my family and for Europe.

One of my colleagues in the department was very likeable and conscientious. In the informal atmosphere of the office I tended to express my views about the way things were done in Brussels fairly forcefully. We got on well. When I started going on about sanctimonious religious people who thought they could purify their souls just by going to church on Sunday, she didn't say anything. But after a while I realised that she was religious and that she practised Christianity in her daily life and not just in church.

My curiosity was aroused. I asked her one day about the pile of letters she was sending through the internal mail. She told me they were invitations to the annual meeting of the Commission's Christian prayer group.

'Prayer group?' I looked at her in astonishment. 'Is there such a thing in the Commission?' It was news to me. At the time I thought of God as something people had invented to avoid taking responsibility for themselves. I couldn't get over the fact that someone as lively and active as she was should be so religious. How could apparently intelligent people with good jobs believe in something like a god? Not only that, their faith was a major influence on their lives. When I started to take an interest, I realised that my colleague would pray before taking virtually any important decision.

It intrigued me and I was determined to find out how someone could justify that to themselves. I bombarded her with questions and gave her a pretty hard time. My colleague was fairly reticent. It was only when she realised that my interest was genuine and I was not trying to make fun of her that she told me more about what she called her experiences with God. She had not always been a Christian but had made a deliberate choice later in life.

I became more and more interested. I started reading the Bible. The whole thing was quite new to me but I could not get over it. It appealed to me.

After that I gradually went through a stage of personal growth and began to regard myself as a Christian. I started going to Church regularly, usually to the Anglican Church in Brussels. My faith has supported me ever since. In my work at the Commission it gave me the courage I needed, especially when I decided to take some action.

Impenetrable Set-up

I certainly needed some support in DG XXII, where the whole set-up was fairly impenetrable. At the time there were a number of major European programmes in operation. There was first the Leonardo da Vinci programme for vocational training and further training in the European Union. Then there was the Socrates educational programme and lastly the Youth programme. All these programmes focused a great deal on international exchanges, the development of multi-media educational aids and language teaching. Outside contractors, known as TAOs, helped the Commission to run the programmes.

To coordinate all these activities more effectively, a good communication and information network was needed. It was decided to set up a computer network with an on-line link between DG XXII, the TAOs for the Leonardo and Socrates programmes and all the national agencies for the two programmes and the youth programme in the Member States. A steering group was to supervise the setting-up of the network.

As a member of the NETY (Network for Education Training

and Youth) steering group, when I attended the meetings I became more and more amazed at what was happening. The outside office that was supposed to be setting the network up for us was simply not up to the job. The selection procedure was unclear and when it came to performance all kinds of problems arose and there were disagreements about how to resolve them. The outside office even brought in members of the European Parliament to put pressure on DG XXII. In the end the office withdrew from the project without finishing the job. It had already been paid a large part of the fee, but none of it had to be paid back. There were rumours circulating that one or more European officials were involved with the firm.

The delivery of the network kept being postponed and the parts already in operation had all kinds of defects. The technology used was quickly outstripped by the rapidly developing Internet. Over the next few years it was a source of frustration for everyone who had to use it.

At one of our departmental meetings with our head of unit there was slightly embarrassed laughter at the way a contract was awarded to a consultant. A Professor Pneumann, who had a very close relationship with Edith Cresson's cabinet, was apparently a very suitable choice for this job. Since Professor Pneumann had already been working on it for some time, the official concerned had few illusions about the whole tender procedure.

'A waste of time,' he called it. 'We all know Pneumann has already got the contract sewn up'.

The head of unit was not so sure. 'You never know who is going to put in a tender. In any case we have to go through the procedure properly. I'll only go along with it if the choice of Pneumann can be justified on paper'.

The official concerned looked at him rather pityingly and we went on with the agenda.

Too Much Work?

Things started to look up when, in 1997, plans were made for a major internal review, to be carried out by a leading international audit firm. The review was intended as a basis for reorganisation. Its brief was to look at the division of responsibilities between the TAOs and DG XXII. A number of functions currently performed by the TAOs were to be transferred to the DG. On the other hand it might be more appropriate for others to stay with the TAO. The aim was to allocate all existing and new responsibilities as efficiently as possible within the DG.

But we officials soon began to suspect a hidden agenda. It looked very much as though the exercise was actually to be used as a pretext for taking on a lot more staff in DG XXII in a very short period. The justification for this was that after the rapid growth of the past few years our DG, which was a relatively new one, had to operate very complex and wide-ranging programmes. Apart from that the DG would have more work after the scaling down of the TAOs (of which, incidentally, there was no sign).

Officials also had their doubts about the way in which the contract had been awarded for the review. The leading audit firm had apparently managed to win the research contract worth about £50,000. But no one knew anything about an open invitation to tender, which should have been issued beforehand. The consultancy contract was shown in the books as a 'strategic study' to be carried out under a 'framework contract' for the computer department, which was a somewhat unorthodox way of going about it.

The project manager, listed as a highly-paid senior consultant for the accountants, was selected on the basis of his Commission experience, although as it turned out he had only been on a training attachment. The accountants had investigated the activities of a TAO previously. The report was highly critical of the TAO and as a result this outside contractor was sacked. The accountants then took over the work from the competitor they had got rid of, so that they were now the TAO for the project. It certainly did not seem to me or my colleagues that they had behaved very ethically.

The research methods also left a lot to be desired. The questionnaire used in the surveys was clearly designed for a commercial company and was not suited to a government organisation. It talked about sales departments and production units. It was not clear how and why the questions had to be answered. No time-writing was used and no instructions were given, so the completion of the forms bore no relation to the reality. They were all based on a theoretical working week plus acceptable overtime. Then the work was divided up retrospectively over the period. If you then put down the work you had not got round to, the net result was always that more staff were needed. In spite of the criticisms, no effort was made to alter the research method.

That was what made us suspect that the whole exercise was designed to create more jobs in the DG and not to increase efficiency as we had been told.

We were not given enough time to fill all the forms in properly. The data were not checked carefully. Each unit—and indeed each member of staff—had their own ways of dealing with the survey.

Inevitably the results that this produced were highly inaccurate and impossible to compare. Everyone was incensed at the poor standards and complained openly about it in the hierarchy, but still we all had to go along with it. Most people complied reluctantly, but some units sabotaged the operation by not filling in the forms at all or filling them in late. I was supposed to put together all the data for the overall survey for our unit, which was obediently cooperating. At first I complied, but after a while I refused to carry on. I wrote a memo setting out all our objections. All that happened was that they stopped bothering me with the research and worked around me. It was that review that made me decide to rejoin the union, because if I was going to take such an intransigent attitude it might get me into trouble.

Colleague With a Problem

I had a good relationship with a Flemish colleague in DG XXII, an in-house accountant called Erik Bonders. When I met him in 1997, Erik had only been with the Commission for a year. Before that he had worked in one of the big international audit firms. He was critical of the Commission's accounting; we soon realised we had that in common. We chatted about some of the gossip that was going around the DG, but that was about all.

Around September 1997 I went to see him. He worked on the top floor. I needed to lose some weight so I used the stairs from the fourth floor. Even a little bit of exercise was worth it. By the time I got to his office I was out of breath. Something seemed to be bothering Erik, but apparently he didn't want to talk about it. Maybe it would do him good to get out for a bit. We went to a snack bar a couple of streets away with another colleague.

It was an interesting lunch. Erik told us what was on his mind. He had done an audit at the TAO for the Leonardo programme and had come across all kinds of irregularities and abuses. What he had managed to uncover was pretty serious. There were clearly grounds for a further investigation, but it would probably be very sensitive politically. He was particularly worried that he would not get enough support to enable him to bring these findings out into the open.

Erik was a man of integrity. He was in an awkward predicament. He had done his work honestly and conscientiously, but probably nothing would come out. I knew exactly how he felt. There were so many other funny things going on in the Commission that people talked about, but the officials responsible did nothing about them. It would not do their careers any good. That had already been made plain in 1995 when Bernard Connolly, a British senior official in the economic affairs DG had gone on record about his frustration at the way in which EMU (Economic and Monetary Union) was being introduced. He was immediately sacked.

Collecting the Evidence

Nothing was going to change that way. The European institutions, with all their good intentions, would eventually come to grief through their own mismanagement.

If you wanted to achieve anything with your criticisms, then you had to be well-prepared. At that point I decided to show Erik that he was not alone. So I began compiling my own dossier with all the indications of irregularities, abuses, fraud and corruption that I could find.

The file started with a few loose memos if I came across any contracts that looked slightly dubious or colleagues told me over coffee about things that particularly bothered them. A little while later I began collecting evidence systematically. I tried to follow up clues and began searching actively in the computer system for contracts for specific contractors who were suspect. I confronted colleagues who had from time to time let something slip and asked them what they were going to do about it. Mostly they didn't answer but sometimes they told me more and decided that something really should be done about the situation. Occasionally I was able to look at the files or people would let me have copies of them.

The stack of evidence grew bit by bit but I still didn't know at that stage what I was going to do with all this information. At any rate I knew I had to have conclusive proof before I could go and see anyone with it.

When I was going through our unit's internal network and correspondence I came across some interesting correspondence. I also found a few things in the files that colleagues showed me. I later realised that at some stage a policy initiative by Edith Cresson had been virtually assigned the status of a European programme. This was the White Paper on education and vocational training, written on Mrs Cresson's initiative and approved by the Commission at the end of 1995. Not being a European programme it did not have to go through Parliament and consequently had no separate budget. Even so it was clear that the objectives had to be achieved regardless of cost. These included the introduction of a computerised Europe-wide knowledge evaluation system, the promotion of adult education, the teaching of a second foreign language (and guess which language that would have to be for most Europeans?) and the establishment of a European volunteer service.

A number of (groups of) contractors were invited to submit project proposals. These were mainly French institutions. DG XXII and Mrs Cresson's cabinet supervised the project proposals in order to guide them through the selection procedures for programmes such as Leonardo and Socrates. Money was only available under these programmes, which had been approved by the Council of Ministers and the Parliament. There was even a letter suggesting changes in the way the project proposals were presented so that the international selection committee would not know they were nearly all French initiatives.

As I delved into the files and records, it struck me that

Brussels is a very small world. It was remarkable how certain names cropped up again and again. For instance I found contractors who worked on similar contracts for various DGs. The DGs did not check properly, so there was a risk of double financing. Even more disgracefully I found relatives in positions—for instance in TAOs and DGs—where they could give each other preferential treatment.

Supportive Colleagues

You might think that sifting through documents looking for irregularities would be a secretive exercise that had to be done on the quiet. But that was not how I approached it. Right from the start I was open about it. I didn't take any documents without telling my colleagues and I let them know what I was up to. After all I was trying to make our organisation more transparent. Anything that would not stand up to scrutiny had to be brought out into the open and then done away with.

Although some of my colleagues appeared somewhat amused at my sense of justice, some were more appreciative of my efforts. Others were relieved that they could at last get it off their chests and be taken seriously. Occasionally people who had been openly sceptical about my detective work later gave me important information.

One day I met a colleague, Lars Sorensen, in the corridor. He looked at me mockingly. 'How's it going, Paul? You look busy again. What are you up to now?'

I felt a bit uncomfortable. He seemed to be implying that I was a busybody. We were going the same way but I didn't really feel like talking, not in that tone at any rate. I answered a bit grudgingly, 'You know very well. I'm always on about things that are not right and I intend to do something about them'.

'But that's not your job,' he said disapprovingly. 'That's what we have auditors for. Think about it, if everyone went on like you do we'd never get any work done'.

I looked at him. Should I start arguing with him and tell him that the auditors would never be able to get hold of the right information? I didn't think that was a good idea.

'You know, Lars, I have been working on this for quite a while and you know as well as I do that there are things happening in our DG that are not right. It's time someone did something about it. I'm not going to do anything stupid. But someone has to say something!' The last sentence came out rather vehemently because I was still wondering whether that someone should be me.

'What can you do?' Lars asked me.

I hesitated a minute. 'Well, I could for instance go and talk to Financial Control, I do know a couple of people there'.

He laughed. 'And do you think they're going to listen to you? Well, you obviously know that yourself. But usually these things end up badly'. He suddenly looked at me anxiously.

'But you speak out when you think things need changing', I replied. I was referring to his activities in the gay rights movement.

Lars was a bit annoyed. 'That's completely different, you can't compare the two'.

I made a despondent gesture and prepared to leave.

'We'll have to meet for a coffee some time', Lars said as I went off along the corridor.

A couple of days later Lars Sorensen phoned me. He spoke in the same mocking tone. 'Hello Paul, Lars here. Still just as busy?'

'No, everything's fine', I muttered non-committally.

'Listen, we'll have to go and have a coffee. Have you got a moment now?

I happened to be between two jobs, so I went. As I was going downstairs I wondered why Lars wanted to meet me for coffee. I was well aware that I was not particularly interesting company for him. We had coffee and chatted about this and that. As we were going upstairs again he asked if I would come with him for a minute. In the office he turned round and shut the door. What was going on?

He looked at me. I looked back, a bit confused. Then Lars went over to a cabinet. 'Paul, if you're still working on that, I might have something else for you'. He got out a file.

'Just have a look, I don't know if you can do anything with it. But I think it might interest you'.

I was surprised and at the same time very curious. He opened the file. 'It's correspondence and reports on the "cellule de communication"'.

'What's that?'

Lars was evasive and put the file quickly into my hands. 'See for yourself. It was one of the new ideas from Mrs Cresson's office, Ladoreur was in charge. It's all in there.'

He looked at me triumphantly. I must admit that I had not expected anything like that from him. I had a quick look in the file.

'How did you get hold of it, Lars?'

'At the beginning I used to go to some of the meetings. One of my colleagues was very closely involved with it. As I said, I don't know if it's any use to you, but just have a look at it'.

I swung the file happily. 'I certainly will. At least you've come up with something concrete!' I said. He had told me nothing and then all of a sudden he was giving me hard facts. He had obviously had a reason for keeping the file; I was curious as to what I would find in it.

I thanked him and took the documents away.

'Don't forget to let me have it back quickly, Paul', he said at the door. I promised I would.

When I got back to my office I looked through the file. At first sight the minutes of meetings, internal memos and other documents did not seem to be anything out of the ordinary. I photocopied the documents and returned the original to Lars.

It was only when I looked through the papers quietly later that I realised how valuable the information was. I felt a surge of adrenaline. This file was just what I needed. It explained how a 'cellule de communication' had been set up for Commissioner Cresson. The first minutes of meetings dated from early 1995, just after Mrs Cresson was appointed commissioner. The meetings were attended by members of Madame Cresson's personal staff and senior officials from DG XII (scientific research), DG XIII (telecommunications research), the JRC (Joint Research Centre) and DG XXII, where I worked. Ladoreur, at one time Mrs Cresson's chef de cabinet, was in charge of the first meeting. A communication unit was to be set up, operating under the direct control of the cabinet. The unit was to have jurisdiction over the whole of Mrs Cresson's field of responsibility: research, education, vocational training, innovation. According to the minutes a small number of outside communications experts would assist the unit initially in establishing what was needed and then drawing up the tender specifications for the selection of communications firms.

So far so good, but later on I came across a name that was vaguely familiar. A letter dated 19 May 1995 mentioned that a contract was being drawn up for an outside expert, Louise Recivieur. I stopped reading. Where did I recognise that name from?

The name kept cropping up. Mrs Recivieur appeared to have been a member of the unit more or less from the start up until the time the tender specifications were published. Could there be something wrong with that?

I started looking more closely and leafed through the framework contracts from our department. I couldn't believe my eyes. A firm in Paris by the name of Mayonic Public Relations had won the contract. The Mayonic contract was signed Mrs. Louise Recivieur, chairman of Mayonic. I compared the data and the details again very carefully. There was no doubt: Mrs Recivieur had been involved personally in the tender specifications and had then won the contract herself. That was totally against the rules. Almost unbelievable.

I looked for the name Mayonic in our records. The firm appeared to have received no less than £180,000 in payments from the Commission. Again I saw the name Recivieur crop up in the computer system, this time as the 'contact' at the contractors, Mayonic.

When I looked through the file again a couple of days later I noticed that the chef de cabinet Mr Ladoreur was directly involved in planning, management and procedures in the 'cellule de communication' in the initial phase. He wrote letters to departments, proposed that outside experts should be brought in and stipulated that those same experts should be involved in the tender specifications. I began to wonder how the other six tender procedures had been run. All seven contracts had apparently been awarded to firms in Brussels or Paris. Obviously you had to be a French speaker to work for Mrs Cresson's unit.

Time Bomb

In the meantime Erik Bonders had told me about the enormous problems he had had both during and after the audit of the Technical Assistance Office for the Leonardo da Vinci programme. At the beginning of October 1997 the first complete draft of his audit report on the Leonardo TAO was ready. I had not read it, but I thought that from what Erik had told me the report could cause a revolution.

In the audit Erik had come across careless mistakes in the invoicing and calls for tender. There was also evidence of fraud and favouritism that went completely beyond the pale. That was all in Erik's report. The report was bound to be a time bomb. But who was going to detonate it? I did not see the report beforehand.

The draft report had to be read first of all by Erik's head of unit, Mr Petit, and Mr McKinsey, the Director-General. After that, radio silence. There was no official comment and the report was not approved. Erik was told to go and talk to the management at the Leonardo Technical Assistance Office. At a series of meetings the TAO managers, Erik Bonders and Erik's head of unit, Mr Petit, discussed how the audit findings were to be interpreted. To Erik's dismay his head of section consistently took the side of the TAO manager, Mr Quicheron. Erik challenged Quicheron about the invoices that had been paid without any work or contracts, but Petit openly questioned his colleague's findings and gave Quicheron another chance to come up with some work reports. Quicheron pleaded that work reports could be accidentally mixed up and Petit agreed that that could easily happen. Some of the reports that Quicheron later produced as the work of the outside consultants submitting the invoices had been written internally by staff at the Leonardo TAO and not by the consultants at all. Erik had proof of this from the TAO staff themselves, who showed him the records on a computer in the TAO. Some of the people at the Leonardo TAO had been unhappy for quite a while about what was going on. Erik was able to use their specific inside information to support many of his arguments at the meetings.

The negotiations were very difficult for Erik, firstly, of course, because he had no backing from his own superiors. Petit more or less left him in the lurch in the discussions. The TAO was also known to have good contacts in Mrs Cresson's private office (cabinet). Was Erik going to have to fight a losing battle on his own?

He decided it was better to be safe than sorry and toned down some of his findings, mainly where he suspected fraud but could not actually substantiate it. Staff at the TAO had told him all kinds of stories but he could not use their statements. They were anxious to remain anonymous for fear of reprisals. Too many people who made a nuisance of themselves had been sacked from the TAO in the past.

Nonetheless Erik Bonders stood by many of the allegations in his report at the end of 1997. He also specifically recommended that since the audit findings were so serious a copy of the report should be sent to Financial Control (DG XX) and UCLAF. At that stage, however, the report was still only in draft form. Until his superiors had approved it, Erik had to keep it quiet. It had no status and he had to obey his superiors. The draft report stayed in the drawer. Would it ever emerge? At any rate the information did not get to Financial Control or to UCLAF, so they were unable to take any action.

A Job For UCLAF?

I considered reporting the matter to the Commission's fraud prevention unit, UCLAF. I had no idea how much opposition there would be. At that point I was still unaware that two other DG XXII officials had already been to UCLAF earlier that year. I only learned about this a year later. I was told by another colleague, René Lejeffe, that he had approached UCLAF several times about irregularities in DG XXII and he complained to me that they were not prepared to take any action.

Nevertheless I took the plunge. I had already collected plenty of information and I wanted to go to UCLAF and find out if they would start an investigation into the irregularities in DG XXII. To begin with I phoned Guus, a Dutchman I knew who worked in UCLAF. He was very reliable but could sometimes be a bit long-winded. He greeted me enthusiastically. 'Hello Paul, it's ages since I've heard from you, how's it going?'

'Fine thanks, how about you?' I came quickly to the point. 'The reason I'm ringing is that you work for UCLAF and I have a problem that I would like to discuss with someone in UCLAF. You're about the only person I know there and I thought you might know someone who can be trusted'

'Well, everyone at UCLAF has to be trustworthy, you know that. It's not easy to get in'. Guus was very proud of his job at UCLAF.

'Yes Guus, I realise that, but I am dealing with something very sensitive here and it might even go up as far as the Commissioner's private office. I don't want to find myself with someone who doesn't know how to keep his mouth shut. We're only human, aren't we, after all?'

Guus was a bit piqued. 'Come on, Paul, that is why we're in UCLAF'. He patiently explained to me that UCLAF was receiving sensitive information all the time and so the confidentiality of the information was guaranteed. He gave me the name of the person in UCLAF I should talk to.

'OK, thanks', I said. 'But I'd rather have a chat with someone first of all about it. Someone who isn't French'.

Guus thought that was ridiculous. 'Just because someone's French it doesn't mean he can't deal with anything to do with the French commissioner. Can you imagine what it would be like?' However Guus did give me the name of a contact, although slightly under protest. I thanked him and promised to explain it to him in more detail later.

At home I told Edith that I was going to talk to UCLAF behind my bosses' backs. Edith was worried and wondered if I should do that. 'Do you really have to? Aren't you stirring up trouble for yourself?'

I reassured her. 'I'm not actually going to tell any wild stories and immediately call for an investigation. I'm only going to have an informal chat with someone from UCLAF. I just want to know what they think of it all'.

Edith was not reassured. 'Don't do anything rash, Paul'.

'I do know what I'm doing', I assured her, but I was beginning to have doubts myself. You don't just go along to UCLAF. I was actually going to 'grass' on my own colleagues. But then I thought again about the files on DG XXII, by now a large pile, and about the colleagues who had helped me with them.

Soon after that I had an informal meeting with Carlo Bianchi, the UCLAF official whose name I had been given. I took the underground to the UCLAF building in a Brussels suburb. Guus met me there and we had a sandwich in the canteen first. A while later Guus introduced me to Bianchi, an Italian about the same age as me with penetrating eyes. In his office he gave me a steady and searching look. 'Guus told me you wanted to have a talk because you suspect there are some irregularities where you work', he began.

I avoided his eyes. I broke out in a sweat. It was at that moment that I realised there was no going back. Until then I had been able to nose around informally and talk about it with colleagues, but now I was at UCLAF. Playtime was over; now it was getting serious. I swallowed once and out it all came.

I told him about my discoveries, about Professor Pneumann, about the cellule de communication and the abuses at the Leonardo da Vinci TAO.

From time to time Bianchi interrupted with questions. Were these just suspicions or did I also have documents? I realised that my story must sound completely incoherent and wondered what Bianchi thought of it. It was impossible to tell. His expression was totally deadpan. To back up my story I showed him a couple of documents I had on me. For instance I showed him the correspondence between Edith Cresson's private office and DG XXII about the selection of projects in Leonardo and Socrates. I showed him the passages which proved that the rules had not been followed when the contractors were selected.

Bianchi listened quietly and made notes. At the end of the conversation he promised me he would look into it and let me know the outcome. I called in to see Guus and then took the underground back to the centre where I worked.

I didn't really know what to think about it. At any rate I had taken an important step. At the same time I realised that I needed even more evidence. I planned to go on working on it.

So I threw myself into my report again. I uncovered more and more, but everything went quiet. Time went by and nothing happened. We officials knew that the irregularities could easily still be going on.

I heard nothing from UCLAF.

I contacted Bianchi again. He made it clear to me that my information was not concrete enough for them to start an official investigation. I was puzzled. How concrete did it have to be?

Bianchi told me that hard and exhaustive evidence was needed before such high-ranking officials could be investigated.

'But isn't an UCLAF investigation supposed to collect the hard evidence?' I burst out. I found UCLAF's excessive caution hard to understand. Evidently the fraud prevention unit couldn't decide for itself when an investigation was necessary. A department like that inside the Commission could not take an independent stand. I felt let down. UCLAF had admittedly given me a sympathetic hearing, but apparently I had to provide all the evidence cut and dried. That was not my job and I had already devoted too much of my spare time to it. Edith had had enough of me sitting at my computer night after night working on my files.

Edith: 'Paul spent a lot of evenings working on his files at home, in the hope that if they were only complete enough and well substantiated enough common sense would per-suade people to act. At home it had become a routine. After dinner Paul would disappear into his study to carry on with his relentless search. Sometimes after hours of going through the files he would discover a link between people and addresses that shouldn't have been there. He was amazed that it was all so easy and that no one felt compelled to do anything about it. I kept asking him to give it up but Paul could not just stand by and watch and later I understood why. When he told me about it I thought I understood his anger and frustration.

He uncovered more and more things that were truly bewildering. It was apparently just accepted that the Commission's DGs were sometimes run by people with no sense of decency or respect for "the European ideal". Now that I am an "insider" whether I like it or not, I won-der how isolated he must sometimes have felt. His dogged search revealed more and more suspicions and proof. More and more colleagues revealed things to him that they had also discovered. They stood by and looked on. I was some-times afraid that people were using Paul to save them hav-ing to do anything themselves'.

CHAPTER FOUR

The Leonardo Affair

As I carried on with my detective work and discovered more and more, I started losing my motivation to go on working in DG XXII. I kept coming across further signs of irregularities and favouritism, especially at the Leonardo TAO. What was so shocking was that almost everyone in the DG knew something about a piece of the jigsaw – or at least had their suspicions –but failed to do anything about it. Or rather they were afraid to do anything about it.

Leonardo was problematic, for two reasons. Firstly because of the culture; the irregularities in the TAO for the Leonardo da Vinci programme were part of a tradition of sleaze. All kinds of abuses had gone on in the earlier Force programme which had preceded Leonardo (also under DG XXII). Secondly the TAO had much too close a relationship with Mrs Cresson's cabinet. Since the person at the very top evidently knew what was going on, many officials feared for their jobs and were afraid to start an active investigation into the Leonardo TAO's activities. It could spell the end of their careers if it came out that very senior officials or even Commissioners had overstepped the mark.

Where it all Began
A bit of digging around in the Force programme files revealed a

damning picture. The TAO for the programme was a subsidiary of Agenor, the same as the TAO for Leonardo. The old audit reports for the Force TAO showed a similar picture to Erik Bonder's draft audit report, which was now lying neglected in a drawer - at least if we let it stay there.

The administration and accounting for many of the Force projects left a great deal to be desired. The contractors painted an over-optimistic picture in their final reports in order not to miss out on further funding. If good products were developed they were not properly distributed, according to the audit reports. The auditors found that several contractors had been paid twice. A contractor would obtain money from two different European programmes to finance the same job. The auditors at Force also came across fictitious transactions and inadequate proof of the legal status of contractors. For instance some sub-contractors simply used accommodation addresses. The auditors even suggested drawing up a blacklist with the names of contractors who were attempting to defraud the system. Contractors often tried to keep Force products developed with EU aid for themselves in order to sell them later at commercial prices, when it is one of the specific aims of the European programmes to make products as widely available as possible in Europe. Examples of this were a multi-media programme for language teaching and specialist technical courses. However the conditions for their distribution were not clearly laid down in the contracts. There was also the problem that if European subsidies are used in this way it can interfere with the commercial market for the products. I still remember a colleague's expression of surprise when she told me a friend of hers had paid quite a large sum of money in a shop for a language-teaching computer programme. She recognised the programme as one developed with a subsidy from one of our programmes. We both agreed that the competition was not going to be very pleased about that.

These Force audit reports made the situation absolutely clear but virtually nothing was done in all that time. I found that absolutely shocking. In fact the problems with Leonardo were already going on in Force, which was also run by Agenor. Consequently the Force irregularities carried on just the same under Leonardo. Much later the Committee of Wise Men took a strong view on that in its first report. The committee thought that DG XXII should have taken the Force audits into account in the selection procedure for the Leonardo TAO.

The Leonardo TAO

The Leonardo programme was set up to support vocational training initiatives in the member states. The programme was to cover the period 1995 to 2000 and the estimated total cost was in the region of £400 million. The programme came under the jurisdiction of Commissioner Cresson. DG XXII was responsible for its administration and contracted the work out to a Technical Assistance Office.

At the end of 1994 an open invitation to tender was issued for a TAO to run the programme for DG XXII. Agenor was selected and given a year's contract for the job (renewable). This was a responsible and major assignment. The Leonardo TAO, which in fact was Agenor's only activity, received dozens of project proposals for vocational training annually, from which eventually around 700 were selected each year.

Agenor SA was set up by the French organisation CESI, a non-profitmaking association of trade unions and large firms in France, to promote ongoing training for senior management. Through the supervisory board there was a link to a firm of consultants called SISIE, in which the Schneider company also had shares. Mrs Cresson had been a director of Schneider. It's a small world ...

What Went Wrong

All the investigations carried out into the Leonardo TAO revealed a catalogue of mismanagement.

The Leonardo TAO used a particular firm of printers, *Klavertje Vier* (Four Leaf Clover), to do its printing work. Obviously it was supposed to follow the rules on tendering, but there were ways of getting round these. For instance the printing firm would submit its tenders last and these would just happen to be slightly lower than the most favourable quotation from competitors. On one occasion the TAO altered the application (specifications) to make sure that particular firm got the job. A job would quite often be split into smaller orders, so that an invitation to tender was not necessary and the order could be placed with *Klavertje Vier* direct. It turned out to be a very small printing firm with only three staff. Probably it contracted the work out to 'genuine' printers and the margin was still profitable enough for it to make a living. It certainly didn't have much else to live on, because the investigations revealed that the orders from the Leonardo TAO probably accounted for 100% of its turnover. So the TAO was the firm's only customer.

With the TAO staff management in particular the system was full of loopholes. At one point a political decision was taken in Belgium to freeze wage increases, but that didn't bother the management and staff of the TAO. All sorts of creative solutions were devised.

While the Force programme was in operation one full-time employee was getting illegal payments as well as his salary. Under Leonardo he put in invoices between 1995 and 1997 for consultancy work that he was supposed to have done for TAO in addition to his regular job. The invoices were on the letterhead of his wife's consultancy firm. In all he was paid nearly £47,000 on top of his normal salary. As well as his salary, the systems manager submitted accounts for £4,700. Apparently there were also illegal salary salary increases to certain members of staff who had shown themselves loyal to the director.

The director and staff regularly went on business trips, mostly to their own countries. The reasons for the trips were not shown in the accounts and there were no reports on them. The auditors got the impression that the trips were simply a way of topping up salaries. Staff could obtain advances and loans from the TAO just like that, or even write cheques in their own name. And remember, the TAO was run entirely on European funds.

The TAO's director, Mr Quicheron, was given too much latitude to run things his own way. Large invoices could be paid just on his say-so. His wife was head of administration and personnel for the TAO. She had started at her husband's TAO as a secretary earning £1,400 a month, but within two years had worked her way up to head of department on a salary of £3,500. A meteoric rise! Their future daughter-in-law had also started as a secretary but became head of the project selection department, increasing her salary at a stroke from £1,700 to £2,400. Another very nice promotion in the Leonardo TAO family firm!

Since there was no system of auditing sales and purchases apart from the director's authority, the accounts were able to develop into a testing ground for irregularities. The auditors came across all kinds: accounts for work not authorised by the Commission, invoices for work that had probably never been done with references to reports that had never been written, false invoices, invoices for phantom experts, accounts for consultancy work for which no contract had been drawn up, invoices with no proof of delivery, invoices for amounts that bore no relation to the work done.

One example of excessive expenditure was the annual payment of £40,000 sterling to the University of Exeter in

England for consultancy. This was based on a daily fee of no less than £1,700 for Sir Rodney Netherby, a professor at the university, which had never been approved by the Commission.

Transfer to Financial Control

In the summer of 1997 I ran into a senior official from Financial Control outside work. At an earlier meeting he had remarked on my thoroughness and said in passing that I could always apply to his DG because they needed people like me. I was pleasantly surprised when he mentioned it again, but didn't really know what to think and didn't pursue it.

In DG XXII I came up against more and more irregularities and consequently more opposition. The longer I worked there, the more I would indirectly be helping to fill other people's pockets. It was clearly high time DG XXII was cleaned up. At the same time I knew the obstacles that colleagues with integrity like Erik Bonders were faced with and so, when a few posts fell vacant in Financial Control's Internal Audit division in the autumn, I saw my opportunity.

Internal Audit was an unusual unit within Financial Control, for several reasons. Not only did it carry out regular audits in all the Commission's departments, it also worked on special investigations when irregularities were suspected. I would certainly feel at home there. I applied and was accepted.

I secretly hoped that in Financial Control I would have a chance to take part in an investigation into the irregularities in DG XXII in relation to the Leonardo TAO and Mrs Cresson's cabinet. Funnily enough, after a lot had come out into the open Mrs Cresson publicly alleged that I had been dismissed from DG XXII for incompetence!

Edith: 'Paul went to work in Financial Control, back to the work with which he had already had a love-hate relationship for so many years. Careers guidance tests always showed that he had an aptitude for this kind of work, but Paul never wanted to believe that. Even so you can't go against nature. He had already moved from one DG to another in the Commission several times, usually when, as a budget manager, he had come up across things that didn't look right. It never ceased to amaze him how highly-paid people in senior positions schemed to get even more money or give relatives or friends opportunities to make money. This was often done with the connivance of Commission officials, who just stood and looked on'.

Battle Commences

When I began my new job I started pressing right from the beginning of 1998 for a special investigation into DG XXII. Erik Bonders had already exposed a little of what was going on in the Leonardo TAO, but obviously the rest was not going to come out. Although Bonders had said in his draft report the previous year that DG XX and UCLAF should be informed as quickly as possible so that the situation could be further investigated, nothing came of it. I wrote letter after letter and urged that an audit should be carried out as Erik Bonders had recommended in his report.

At first no one took much notice. My head of unit thought I had a fixation on my previous DG and he was reluctant to get caught up in the whole thing. It was understandable enough; he wanted to find out first which way the wind was blowing. 'Let me have a look at the report to start with', he said.

There was more trouble then, because officially Erik Bonders' report did not even exist. It was still in draft and had not been approved. I now knew more or less what was in the report, but I couldn't do anything about it without permission.

I tried to persuade Erik to leak it. 'Come on, Erik, you can't just leave it at that. It's a disgrace. I can understand why you couldn't give me the report while I was still in DG XXII, but surely you can now I'm in Financial Control?' Eventually, a month later, my colleagues unexpectedly got hold of the report. It made quite an impression. Now people in my DG were going to take the whole thing a bit more seriously.

But my head of unit still had cold feet. 'That's not the right way to go about it, Paul. I can't do anything about it like this. I have to get hold of a copy of the report officially'.

I have no time for red tape. It was almost unbelievable. But I knew he was right; without the report he could not ask for a special investigation. How was he going to get hold of the report through normal official channels?

Then I realised that the report had been produced in a routine investigation. If my head of unit had the plan for this, he could ask for the 'usual' report. I looked in the records and luckily an application had actually been made to our DG at the time for an audit, which had to be done under the rules. So we could ask for the report.

I also wanted UCLAF to get a copy of Bonders' report.

'Erik, it's now or never. It can't go on like this. You can see that no one's taking any action. Are you just going to stand by and do nothing while your work is swept under the carpet?' I put forward every argument I could think of to persuade Erik to go to UCLAF. I knew he felt bitter because nothing had been done about his report. All the abuses were just being allowed to carry on. What was the point of him doing all that work?

Finally he agreed to go and see Bianchi in UCLAF. But he was a dutiful employee and wanted to do it by the book, so at first he did not show them the draft report.

However there was no response from UCLAF. They

continued to maintain that they did not have enough proof to be able to start an investigation.

Time went by. Erik's report had still not come out officially. In the meantime the rumours had started. Everyone knew there was something fishy about the Leonardo TAO and that I was openly calling for an investigation, preferably a special investigation with no prior warning. Fortunately we were acquiring more and more allies who were also prepared to act. Like us, they felt that the cautious and bureaucratic approach was getting nowhere. But we had no other option than to keep working through official channels. One of my colleagues in my new DG, Pim de Kraker, took the initiative from me. He wanted Bonder's report brought out. His head of unit was against it; he was afraid of trouble with another DG and preferred to stay out of it. De Kraker stuck his neck out and took a risk by sending a copy of his urgent request to the management. His head of unit was forced to go after the draft report, which he did.

I later heard that Mr Petit in DG XXII went to a lot of trouble to find out how we knew of the report's existence. Obviously he would have preferred to keep it hushed up.

More Surprises

Now I was working in Financial Control, I received even more information about abuses. Colleagues gave me files to look at or told me where I could find the right documents. I found out about irregularities that I had had no idea were going on. I thought of Erik Bonders' report, which would have still been on ice if I had not done anything, and I knew I had no choice but to carry on.

I searched and put things together and I found some evidence. I checked through the computer system, analysed payment summaries, sometimes sat all night at the computer or

searching on the Internet. I also interviewed colleagues informally. I found out that Agenor had set up a TAO especially for
Leonardo programme before this programme had been
announced publicly. It had already been working on the Force
programme and had prepared for the contract well beforehand—
and actually won it. Was that chance? Not according to some of
the TAO staff. They told me that Agenor's selection in the TAO
tendering procedure had been rigged. Agenor had not really
scored better on the actual technical assistance criteria, but it did
get a higher score for policy advice by a permanent group of
experts which it had assembled for that purpose. However their
expertise had very little to do with assistance in running a programme. The head of the Finance unit, François Petit, was on the
selection committee at the time and apparently manipulated the
selection table in that direction.

Agenor's salary records were found to be incorrect. Social
security inspectors discovered in an inspection that Agenor had
not complied with the social security regulations and demanded
an extra payment.

The flows of money at the Leonardo office were not at all
clear. For instance I saw a copy of a fax from a major bank, con-
firming to Agenor that a sum equivalent to about £95,000 had
been transferred to a German university. As far as I knew there
was no contract with this university that matched this payment
and I could find no other reason for the payment.

In December 1995, before the call for tenders had even been
announced, Mrs Cresson had already been in personal contact
with one of the candidates for the 1996 Leonardo programme.
This was an institute at the University of Poitiers, very close to
Chatellerault where Mrs Cresson was mayor. She introduced
Professor Pneumann to the institute. Later on the university
responded to an invitation and actually submitted a project

proposal, which was accepted at the end of 1996.

There were rumours that the contractors working on the Leonardo programme or their staff had worked on projects together before or had vague personal or business connections. Often this went hand in hand with shoddy accounting. For instance VEBO, until 1995 a one-man business set up by a Dutch provincial politician, had contracts for three different DGs, including DG V and DG XXII, and at least nine European programmes. VEBO was also involved in the planning for Leonardo and bid for one of the projects based on Mrs Cresson's White Paper. VEBO did not keep proper accounts; contracts with free-lancers, for instance, were not shown. One of the VEBO project managers was Patricia Etoile, who had already been associated with irregularities in DG V in the past.

Lieven Verstreepe told me that this contractor had put in a new project proposal and asked me for information. We checked the facts. Mrs Etoile had previously worked in DG XXII and Erik Bonders found evidence of her insatiable appetite for work. She had worked on two projects at the same time and in the same period had declared 38 working days a month. The audit of the Leonardo TAO also showed that she still had an old debt outstanding; it was not clear what for. She was not asked to repay the money; instead the debt was written off as irrecoverable for reasons that were not clear. At the time Erik Bonders' head of unit, François Petit, had told him not to put this in his audit report. Why?

Lastly the Leonardo programme produced a further surprise. The auditors had noted that the standard of the projects they had audited was remarkably low. Mrs Cresson had always said in jus-tification that there might be a few 'little administrative prob-lems' but the programme itself was very good. That was simply not true. At any rate it was never investigated in more detail.

Edith: 'Nearly every day Paul had meetings with people over lunch or coffee and a network was beginning to grow up of people who could no longer ignore what they knew. They came from many different departments and also outside the organisation. Papers and information were collected and a clear picture began to emerge of the scale of the irregularities. Lots of phone calls were made, meetings were arranged. Paul was acquiring more and more equipment: a mobile phone, a fax, various address books databases on CD Rom, special recording equipment. It began to look as though he was planning a crime film. I sometimes didn't see Paul for nights on end. He was sitting at his computer. I just left him to it. It was not much fun, but I wasn't going to try and dissuade him'.

TAO Staff Speak Out

Now everything started to happen. Even staff at the Leonardo BAT seemed ready to speak out about what had been going on. I met some of them through Erik Bonders. Eventually I had a number of meetings with various informants, at first with Erik and later on my own, not only at my office but also in restaurants, cafés and stations, in the park and on the underground. When they realised they could trust me the information started to come out—and how!

At one point I had a phone call from one of my informants. As usual I picked up the phone and said, 'Paul van Buitenen'. The person seemed to be phoning from a car; there was a lot of noise.

'This is Sophie. I have got the information ready and I'm on my way back to Brussels. Can we meet this week?'

I quickly got my diary. 'Yes, that would be OK. Do you want to give me the details?'

'All right. We'll meet at one, three, thirteen'. Luckily she remembered to use the code we had agreed.

I had to think about it for a minute, because I still hadn't really got used to this. 'Fine, that's settled', I said and ended the conversation without more ado. Sophie and I had already agreed codes for the place, day and time we were to meet.

Later that week, after I had waited at the rendezvous for nearly half an hour, Sophie drove up. I gestured to an empty parking place, but she beckoned me to get in. She was pleased to see me.

'Aren't we going to the GB restaurant?' I asked her in surprise.

'No', she said, 'I've got a lot to show you and I'm not taking it to the supermarket with me'. She was silent and I wondered where we were going. We drove out of Brussels. At some point we turned off the main road and a couple of minutes later stopped at a square in a village and got out. I was amazed when we started walking towards a bank.

'Do you need to get some money?' I asked her.

'No, we're going inside', she said. 'We can talk quietly there and look at the stuff I have brought for you'. She gave me a triumphant glance and walked across to the counter. She showed the bank clerk a pass and we went downstairs to the safe-deposit. We took off our coats and Sophie opened a large deposit box in the corner, which contained an enormous stack of documents. She began leafing through them quickly and then took out a small pile of papers. 'Here, just read that and tell me what you think'. She gave me the papers and bent over the deposit box again to sort out some documents.

I sat down at a table and began looking through the papers. At first I didn't know where to start, but after a while I realised that this was an entire project file, complete with project proposal, evaluation, correspondence, payments and so on.

Sophie came over and obviously thought I wasn't catching on

quickly enough to what it was about. She pointed out the evaluation forms for the project. Some of them were highly critical but the project had been approved nevertheless. I agreed that this raised questions, but wondered why she thought it so important.

'Don't you get it?' Sophie asked me. 'Everyone thinks that it is just the accounts that are being fiddled at the TAO. But this proves there's much more to it than that'.

I had a feeling she was right, but still didn't really understand why. Impatiently, Sophie explained further. 'About 9 million euros go through the TAO's accounts every year for its operations. If you mess around with that it's peanuts. If politicians are involved then we're talking about something much bigger! Just remember that the TAO manages 100 million euros a year for project subsidies. That's where things go wrong. This project shows that there are fiddles going on within the 100 million too. The choice of projects is influenced'.

I realised she had a point. I had not looked at it like that before. 'But', I objected, 'one case like this is not enough to make any allegations, is it, even if it does prove what you suspect?' Sophie had obviously been anticipating that and went back to the deposit box. 'Here you are, then', she said. 'If you want more, have a look at this'. She came back with an enormous pile of papers and put them down firmly on my table. As I stood looking at them she got her keys out again and went to another deposit box. She opened the door and pointed to the contents.

'Satisfied now, Paul?' I couldn't believe my eyes. Apparently I was not the only person who had been hard at work. From then on I knew that they would find it difficult to stop us.

So my sources eventually provided me with secret information which I began to go through painstakingly. Even now I have still not managed to read it all.

I persuaded some of my former colleagues in DG XXII and

staff of the Leonardo TAO to come and make statements to my head of unit and a few colleagues in Financial Control about the irregularities in DG XXII and the TAO.

I was puzzled about the relationships in the TAO. On the one hand there were staff who had been fed up for a long time with what was going on and kept leaking information to me. On the other hand I got the impression that some people were implicated themselves, perhaps had even been blackmailed or threatened. Staff who protested were sacked, or skilfully manoeuvred out. During my months of detective work I discovered that one of the heads of department at the Leonardo TAO had been dismissed on the spot for fraud. She had been allowed to write cheques in her own name and therefore had done something dishonest, so it was easy for the TAO to get rid of her. It was not uncommon at the Leonardo TAO for staff to be able to borrow money in this way, often in the form of an advance from the TAO's budget surplus. Everything at the TAO was obviously so chaotic that staff totally lost sight of where the line was drawn and could be manoeuvred into positions where they were open to blackmail.

It was clear from all this that staff at the TAO who were critical of the way things were done were pinning all their hopes on me. I felt I could not let them down.

At one point another source rang me. Gérard said he had important information for me. Later that day he came to see me in the office. We could do this without being seen, because when I got a signal on the mobile I went out and took my visitor past reception so that he did not have to sign in. My office was on a different floor from the rest of my unit. When Gérard was in my office I shut the door and pulled down the blind on one side. That way no one could see me or my visitor. Gérard carefully got a couple of files out of a big bag he had with him. By then

I had got used to this kind of thing and I waited expectantly.

As I was looking through a file, he started talking. 'You already know, of course, that the accounts at the TAO are a mess'.

'Can't you be a bit more specific?' I asked, because people often said things like that and it did not really help me much.

'Well, the way they take on staff, the pay policy, the budget, the way they ignore Belgian regulations, everything you can possibly think of', he said, taking a seat. He looked at me with an anxious expression and was obviously uncomfortable. I decided not to criticise but just to let him talk.

'Just give me few examples, then', I suggested.

'How about this?' he said, pointing to one of the pages that he had unfolded. 'This is a good example of how things are done in the TAO. The whole budget is set out in detail in these tables. The totals and the annual budget surplus are absolutely correct'.

I went and stood next to him and looked at the table. Under the heading 'personnel' was a list of all the TAO staff, followed by the salary costs. 'You see this amount here', Gérard went on to explain, pointing to a figure at the bottom right on the next sheet. 'That is the estimated budget surplus for this year. Obviously Quicheron doesn't want that, the money has to go'.

I saw that the amount was nearly £450,000. 'Now, turn over a couple of pages to the same tables and what do you see?' He didn't wait for an answer. 'The surplus has turned into a deficit. Neat, eh?' He looked at me expectantly, so I asked him, 'How did Quicheron manage that?'

'I have found out all about it for you. Look at this!', he said decisively. He picked up a sheet of paper that had been put carefully into a sleeve like a piece of parchment. He held it up triumphantly and then put it down in front of me. The table on this sheet was the same as on the first one but now it had handwritten amendments on it. It was true. The budget surplus had disappeared. 'And what do you notice about the amendments?'

I quickly looked at all the headings and noticed that salaries had been altered and new amounts added, probably for new contractors. Gérard banged the desk impatiently. 'You see the salary increases?' he said. All at once I realised. I skimmed through the list of names. All the people working with Quicheron got a pay rise: his wife, his future daughter-in-law and many others who were loyal to him. The increases were quite substantial.

I looked at Gérard with a big grin. 'You're right, Gérard, giving your family a salary rise is one thing, but doing it to use up your budget is really a bit much. These documents you've brought are excellent!'

Gérard nodded with satisfaction. 'I suppose you'll be wanting copies, won't you?' I nodded in agreement. He gave me the documents and I quickly went to the photocopier. Relieved that Gérard was not going to hang on to his papers but was actually giving me some practical help, I put them all in a file. I had found another piece of the jigsaw.

Much later I heard from people working at the Leonardo TAO that Quicheron, the director, had threatened them as the investigation got under way. Staff were told they would be sacked or they were forced to resign. One employee, Jeanne d'Arcillon, said in her letter of resignation that her employers, Agenor, did not allow her do her work responsibly. It led to a lawsuit between her and Agenor.

Quicheron was acting like a cornered animal and in the end it worked against him. Staff who had been sacked or threatened by him were all the more willing to speak out and even smuggle out documents with real proof of the abuses.

One sunny spring day in 1998 I went to have lunch with an ex-TAO employee who was said to be blackmailing Quicheron, her former boss. At any rate evidence had been found of payments from Quicheron to her firm which were not clear. I asked her about it straight out, but she told me they were back payments for overtime and special jobs she did when she was still working at the TAO.

Did she still have any TAO records? She told me she had collected a box of evidence but Mrs Quicheron had found it when she was on holiday. The material had been confiscated. 'So I'm sorry, I can't help you'.

I was crestfallen. The evidence had been snatched away when it was within my grasp. I really didn't know what to think. One thing was clear: whoever was right, there was fiddling going on in the TAO on a massive scale.

Delays and Obstacles

> *Edith*: 'Paul really believed that after he moved to Financial Control he would finally be able to expose the abuses, instead of having to stand by helplessly and not be able to do anything. But he soon realised that the official decision to start an investigation was a long slow process and not an energetic decision that led to swift action'.

It was only after long consultations between DG XXII, DG XX and UCLAF that it was decided in February 1998 to have the Leonardo TAO audited, not that anything came of it immediately. When it was finally agreed that the investigation was necessary, the meetings still went on for weeks. Which was the competent department? Who was responsible? Which departments and people should be informed and who should not be told? Who would carry out the audit? I was only allowed to attend one of the meetings.

At a meeting with Financial Control in my own DG I was

the only B grade there; the rest were all senior officials. We discussed one of my letters in which I had given a brief summary of the irregularities in DG XII and the Leonardo TAO. In the letter I had pressed for an audit and warned that the TAO should in the meantime seriously expect to be audited in the near future. With that in mind they were probably now putting their records in order. To make sure that no evidence got lost in the process, I urged that the audit should be started without any warning. Obviously I was well aware that taking them by surprise like that was not the way the Commission usually did things.

Everybody at the meeting considered the facts carefully. Looking around, I felt that for the first time my complaints were being acknowledged. The chairwoman, a director in Financial Control and the only woman present, chaired the meeting calmly and with authority, writing the main points up on a board. She struck me as a sympathetic kind of person.

The decision was actually taken, but by the end of February the audit had still not started. I could hardly conceal my disappointment. Every day was crucial. Who could say what was happening to the evidence at the TAO in the meantime? I heard on the grapevine that Quicheron had already rung François Petit, the head of finance in DG XXII, in a rage and threatened to expose the role of DG XXII and Mrs Cresson's cabinet in various proceedings if the Commission dared to put a stop to the TAO activities or get too close to him. Obviously tensions were rising.

The Leonardo TAO started trying to discredit DG XXII auditors, including Erik Bonders. It said the audit reports were wrong. There should have been more consultation on the results of their spot checks and the standard of the projects themselves was not taken into account. The TAO even insinuated that Erik

Bonders had something to do with a missing report.

At the beginning of March I heard from a member of the TAO staff. A number of files in the TAO had been taken to the basement to be 'sorted out'. According to my contact, they were simply clearing out files that might be incriminating. My informant made an excuse to try and keep back a few files but was not allowed to.

The Audit Starts at Last

It was not until 10 March 1998 that the audit of the Leonardo TAO finally began. Obviously Mr Quicheron was asked just beforehand whether he had any objection to being interviewed. So should I have been pleased about it? I had a feeling we had arrived too late. All kinds of evidence might have been done away with.

To my frustration I found out that I was not going to be allowed to take an active part in the audit. No one knew as much about the situation as I did. I knew exactly the right questions to ask TAO staff in the interviews and I knew what "random" checks should be made on what files. Often I could predict what the audit would uncover in a certain place.

But no, I had to stay out of it. They probably thought I was too caught up in it and could not be objective enough. As if the facts did not speak for themselves.

Luckily Erik Bonders and other colleagues kept me informed in the meantime of how the investigation was progressing. The contact was also useful for them because I could give them some hints and help in various ways. I couldn't let it go; by now I just felt too involved. I could see that it was often made difficult for the auditors to do their work.

I openly continued my campaign, although I always acted within the rules. I wrote letters, solicited and unsolicited, and kept up the pressure on my superiors and on UCLAF. I was a permanent thorn in their sides. Occasionally I got a sympathetic hearing, but often the reverse. At one point my director told me I was no longer required to inform my superiors in writing of any abuses. He also confirmed that neither I nor Erik Bonders nor Lejeffe were allowed to do any auditing.

When it became known at the highest level—via the golf course—that Bonders, Lejeffe and I were still in regular contact, I got into serious trouble. My director wrote me a strongly-worded letter reminding me that I was not allowed to question anyone about the Leonardo audit. I replied that I had merely spoken to them as friends and ex-colleagues, although I rather unwisely said that I had asked their advice and also asked them if their audit reports had already been sent to DG XX.

The director immediately sent a written complaint to my head of unit and the Director-General that I had ignored orders from my superiors. That was a serious allegation because it could lead to disciplinary proceedings.

I had to respond immediately, by writing a letter of course. I said that I reserved the right to carry on talking to my former colleagues. I denied that I had disobeyed instructions; in any case I knew nothing about an agreement that I should not go to DG XXII. I concluded by saying that as a committed employee, auditor and Christian I would always consider I had a duty to advise my superiors if I thought they were making a mistake.

This was typical of the conditions in which auditors like Bonders, Lejeffe and myself worked. We were fighting a losing battle. At that stage Lejeffe more or less dropped out. He could not put up with the stress any more and he was worried about his promotion, which was certainly slow in coming.

Patience is not a Virtue

So the investigation went on. That was the least of it. In the meantime I was fretting, and not just because I was being kept out of it. As time went by the situation became more and more acute. There were all kinds of developments afoot.

In the first place the contract with the Leonardo TAO was due to expire at the end of the summer. As far as I knew, no one had taken that into account. There was no contingency plan for another organisation to carry on the work if necessary. So it looked as though the contract with the TAO would be renewed, whatever the outcome of the investigation. I felt very upset about that because in my eyes it meant that people who had done wrong were being rewarded. And things might get even worse. I heard from Bonders that the TAO had asked for extra funds and had been allocated about £500,000 to extend the Leonardo programme to the new or future member states in Eastern Europe – just when Quicheron had got rid of his budget surplus.

But what was much more important was the start of the approval procedure for the new Leonardo programme in the spring of 1998. Obviously the information on what was going on at the TAO was relevant to the decision.

The Commission was to look at the programme proposal on 20 May. The second phase was a major combined programme with Leonardo, Socrates and the Youth programme extended for the period 2000-2006. However the programme proposal contained features that were exactly the same as those that had encouraged the irregularities under the previous Leonardo programme, including external experts, existing networks, national agencies and in particular the use of a mega-TAO responsible for all the programmes.

I was concerned because there was no sign that the information had got through at that level. Evidently DG XXII, DG XX and UCLAF wanted to keep the dirty washing hidden for as long as possible - and certainly not bother the people at the top with it. The European Parliament had been consistently kept in the dark about the situations in Force and Leonardo, so the MEPs would probably vote in favour of Leonardo II later that year without questions asked. Important information would be withheld, which was a serious omission.

I started wondering again whether I should speak to an MEP myself. It was quite a step, but I was less worried about that than about going to see UCLAF the year before. At UCLAF I had still had the feeling that I was going behind people's backs. If I went to the European Parliament I would be bringing things out in the open and making the situation clear.

How did that come about? When I was still in DG XXII, I had been thinking about it and had decided to ring Nel van Dijk, a Dutch Green Left MEP on the left. I didn't know her but she had the reputation of being fearless. She was not afraid to get involved if necessary. I thought back to our telephone conversation. She answered the phone herself, speaking clearly and forcefully.

I briefly explained to her on the phone what was happening at the Leonardo TAO and what I suspected. She immediately asked how much money the programme was costing. When I told her she sounded slightly disappointed. I felt let down; obviously fraud that involved smaller amounts was not so important. What would you call a small amount anyway? We were talking about thousands of pounds. I changed tack.

'When do you think I should tell someone at the European Parliament?'

'Well, really it's up to you to decide. But listen, I am always ready to take information about abuses seriously'. If I provided her with material she would of course consult me about when she should use it.

I was a bit wary and I put the phone down.

I was now asking myself again the same question I had asked then. What should I do? When was the right time to go to the Parliament?

By then it was May. The investigation was still going on. There was no indication that the Commission or Parliament had received any information about the Leonardo TAO. I felt the situation was becoming really urgent. There was no time to go though the normal official channels and procedures. In the middle of May I sat down at my computer and wrote a direct letter to the cabinets of Commissioner Gradin (anti-fraud), Commissioner Liikanen (budgets), Commissioner Van den Broek (out of courtesy) and Secretary-General Trojan. I explained the situation and asked them to postpone the decision on Leonardo II until the current investigation was over and the details were available.

The only response was an invitation to come to Commissioner van den Broek's cabinet and explain. I went there with a general summary of the Leonardo affair but they were reluctant to accept it. The person in the cabinet who received me was understanding and appreciative, but advised me to go to Commissioner Gradin's and Commissioner Liikanen's cabinets. He warned that in future I should follow the proper procedures if I wanted to keep my job in Financial Control. It would be a pity if that happened, because Financial Control needed people like me. I couldn't understand his reasoning.

Soon after that I got a (well-meant) telling-off from my own Director-General. She reassured me about the decision and the progress of the investigation. No final decision had yet been taken on Leonardo II and this time the information really would be used.

But at the end of May it was decided that the Leonardo TAO

contract with Agenor should be renewed in any case. DG XXII even suggested the normal one-year extension, but the management of my DG restricted it to four months and imposed a number of conditions in view of the findings that were now starting to come to light in the investigation.

At that time the Commission approved Mrs Cresson's proposal for the next phase of the Leonardo, Socrates and Youth programmes, a week late. The total budget for the combined Leonardo II was around £2 billion for the period 2000-2004. I sent an e-mail to my colleagues on the auditing team of the Leonardo TAO, warning them about the risks.

I had allowed myself to be reassured by my Director-General, but much later the Committee of Wise Men, in their first report, deplored the fact that the DGs had kept the Commission and therefore also the European Parliament in ignorance at that stage. They also criticised the DGs for not acting. In their view immediate action should have been taken on the Leonardo TAO after Bonders' audit report, in the autumn of 1997. The situation had already dragged on for a year longer than it should have done.

Edith: 'After that Paul tried to do everything by the book. He wrote letter after letter, everyone was given the chance to respond, or rather to act. Each time he hoped to appeal to people's sense of responsibility and duty, but it got him nowhere. He even wrote to the cabinet of the Dutch Commissioner, Mr Van den Broek, in May 1998 in the hope of getting a hearing. Paul was excited when he was asked to talk to a member of the cabinet. He went nervously off to the meeting early in the morning, wearing his best suit. When he rang me later he was totally disillusioned. He had been told that these matters weren't their responsibility and he would do better to go to Commissioner Gradin or Commissioner Liikanen, which he had already done anyway.

He was also told that he should pay more attention to the rules if he wanted to go on working in Financial Control'.

A Good Report

Fortunately my anxiety about the progress of the investigation was overtaken by events. The audit was very painstaking. Although its scope was much too narrow and the auditors did not get to the bottom of everything, a lot more came to light. The report is the first objective account of what was going on in the Leonardo TAO. One of the most startling findings was the way in which the director threatened members of staff who protested at the situation. The report contained a long list of criticisms and concluded that the office should really be closed down immediately.

The draft report was ready on 17 July 1998. That day the senior auditor took the 300-page report personally to DG XXII's head of finance, François Petit, who was due to go on holiday the following week. Three days later the draft report was also sent officially to DG XXII. Since the findings were so serious, Mr Petit was expected to look at it before going on holiday and give his initial comments. That didn't happen. He went off on holiday and there was no response from DG XXII on the draft report during that period. DG XXII said that Petit was spending the whole holiday writing a response to the report. A month later, on 17 August, DG XXII sent a non-committal note saying that the matter was still being considered. Mr McKinsey, the Director-General of DG XXII, responded a few days later, but still only in general terms. At any rate he did not dispute the findings.

By early September there was still no response. It was an awkward situation. The day my Director-General, Gabriella Speculanti, came back from holiday I took a letter to her office. In it I wrote that it was now really vital that the European Parliament was informed of the audit findings. She had promised me already in May that she would do this when necessary. Another TAO would be set up for Leonardo II and I thought this was the right time to learn from past mistakes.

There was no one in yet on the ninth floor. I did not want the letter to get buried in a heap of post. It was still early, I decided to just wait. At about 9 o'clock Mrs Speculanti's secretary arrived and I gave her the letter. 'Yes, I'll pass it on to her, Mr van Buitenen. But you won't get a reply straightaway. She has a month's post and messages waiting for her'.

I would wait and see. I went back down to my office, not expecting to hear anything for a while. Half an hour later the phone rang. It was Mrs Speculanti in person. She assured me that my letter would be taken very seriously, but asked me to hold on for a while before I did anything further.

In fact she did act very promptly, pressing for a response from DG XXII on the provisional report. A change of management in DG XXII caused further delay. Mr McKinsey had left and a senior official, Michele Trovato, was now acting Director-General. Mrs Speculanti asked her colleague to send his comments on the report to the members of the Commission as well. She asked Trovato what DG XXII planned to do if the contract for the Leonardo TAO came to an end after the four-month extension. I heard on the grapevine that she kept insisting on this point but evidently this did not persuade DG XXII to take any definite action. Mrs Speculanti suggested to him that either the Leonardo TAO contract should be terminated or the TAO's management structure should be drastically improved.

Was it laziness, cynical pragmatism or an inability to grasp the situation? In any event, Trovato came up with an alternative proposal at the end of September: the TAO should simply be allowed to work out the whole period, in other words a full year. After all the Leonardo programme was almost finished and it would not be in its interests to break off the contract now.

At the end of September a lot of meetings took place between the two DGs on the outcome of the report. DG XXII was not disputing the audit findings; that was one good thing. The criticism was now mainly directed at the responsibility of DG XXII in the TAO matter as indicated in the audit report. DG XXII tried to play down the findings from the July report as much as possible. A summary of the report was prepared but the original was not attached to it for reference (as it normally would be).

DG XXII insisted that in the interests of continuity the contract with Agenor should be extended to the end of the Leonardo programme. A compromise was reached: the Leonardo TAO contract was to be renewed for a few more months, but the office would then be audited again. Also a close eye would have to be kept by DG XXII in particular on the TAO management. DG XX had another important question for DG XXII: why did they not ask Agenor to replace the TAO's director? He had after all been seen as one of the main problems and causes.

My colleagues in the auditing team and I found this a very sloppy compromise. How could Mrs Speculanti have let herself be taken in like that? And what on earth was the point of yet another audit when the facts were already plain? As it turned out the audit never took place anyway.

What particularly got me down was that I knew all the problems were still going on in the TAO. As members of the auditing team we had met members of the TAO's staff in secret. You had to laugh about it really; these were exciting meetings in small cafés where we were given information and talked about what was happening. Mostly I was on my own, but on this occasion I was with my colleagues. We met in a café at Brussels–Midi station. Pressure had been put on the TAO staff not to say anything detrimental in interviews with auditors. If they wanted to say anything they had to say it in secret. Apparently some of them felt very intimidated by Quicheron. He did not usually make specific threats, but if they protested he took it out on them. Apart from the usual threats of dismissal there was also specific action such as refusing them leave. We were told that they had to approve the reports on current projects whether or not the projects were going well.

The Anonymous Letter

I kept insisting to my Director-General that Parliament should be informed. The vote on the Leonardo programme was due to take place at the beginning of November and this crucial information must not be withheld from Parliament.

Just at that time someone sent an anonymous letter to the European Parliament and a few senior Commission officials about the abuses at the Leonard TAO. The letter referred mainly to Mrs Cresson's White Paper, the conflicts of interest in the small networks and the commercial marketing of products developed under the Leonardo programme. It also described the political manoeuvring by the Cresson cabinet.

The person who wrote the letter knew his facts. Everyone was mentioned by name. The letter was not entirely negative, though; it also contained suggestions for improving the situation.

The letter had one weakness: it specifically urged MEPs not to vote in favour. The European Parliament is not keen on anonymous letters that attempt to influence how it votes. The letter was particularly troublesome in that it was not simply a malicious attack but a serious background report, obviously written by someone who knew what was going on—probably someone on the inside. Mrs Theato, the chairwoman of the Committee on Budgetary Control, said straightaway that she thought the letter should be ignored if the writer did not have the guts to sign it.

Sitting in the public gallery, I was astonished at Mrs Theato's response. Did she not realise the agonies an official must have gone through before taking such an unorthodox and far-reaching step? It was easy for her to talk, with her parliamentary immunity. However I took what she said to heart. If I was going to pass on any information to Parliament I would have to make it quite clear where it had come from.

Of course everyone thought I had written the letter, but I hadn't. I did have a pretty good idea what was going on. There were plenty of other people who were fuming at the way things were being allowed to drag on at the Leonardo TAO.

A Heated Discussion

My Director-General took things in hand. She told the security office to investigate the leak in our DG. I was of course suspect number one. That put me in a difficult position because I didn't even know what was in the letter and had no idea what I was suspected of. So first of all I had to see the letter. When I got hold of it I found that it contained facts that I had not been aware of up to then. It irked me that this investigation could be set up straightaway whereas an investigation into alleged irregularities and fraud was postponed for months on end. It seemed the Commission thought it more important for abuses to be kept quiet, even if that meant nothing was done about them.

Of course I was called up in front of my Director-General,

Mrs Speculanti. I might have expected that. In fact I had to some extent asked for it by sending her an e-mail telling her the abuses at the Leonardo TAO were still going on. I urged her again to tell the European Parliament, but I also said that I was not the person who wrote the anonymous letter.

Two days before the vote in the European Parliament I went to see Mrs Speculanti. The head of personnel was also there. Mrs Speculanti did not disguise her annoyance. She made it clear that as an official I could not go straight to Parliament. That would be direct political influence and I would be seriously overstepping the mark. I could only report through official channels. The head of personnel backed that up. It was an order. I stood up for myself and told her I was genuinely concerned. She was really angry, interrupted me and asked if I understood.

I agreed that strictly speaking she was right. I told her that up to then I had gone through the normal channels but that had had no effect and I realised I could get the sack.

Mrs Speculanti said that the MEPs were well able to call the Commission to account over Leonardo and they had the means to do so. The initiative did not lie with the Commission. Some time later the Committee of Wise Men took a quite different view, saying in their report that it was up to the Commission to supply Parliament with information that was crucial to the decision-making process at the proper time.

Mrs Speculanti made no secret of the fact that she suspected me of having something to do with the anonymous letter. As far as the irregularities still going on in the TAO were concerned, the office had to solve its own internal problems. All DG XX was required to do was to give an opinion as to whether the TAO should carry on or not. It was up to DG XXII to decide what action to take after that.

The discussion became heated and Mrs Speculanti kept

reminding me that there were formal powers and roles. She asked how we were getting on with the final report, to which I replied that I had been prohibited from having anything to do with it and in fact I was not even allowed to go into DG XXII now. She was surprised at that and said I should go and sort it out through my own line managers and if necessary mention her name. Finally she asked me if I had anything else to say. I told her about a complaint from the director of UCLAF that I had stuck my nose into the affairs of another commissioner. She knew nothing about it. I also complained that my superiors had not been persistent enough about Leonardo, to which she replied rather tartly that she was not willing to listen to complaints like that. 'We in the Financial Control DG are not here to hit out wildly at everyone'.

The Vote

So I was effectively gagged a few days before the vote in Parliament, although the European Parliament's rapporteur did actually do something about the anonymous letter. Mrs Waddington, who was responsible for seeing that Parliament had the necessary information, sought assurances from the Commission that all was well with the Leonardo programme.

President Santer immediately sent her a formally correct but evasive reply playing down the results of the audit. He said there was an internal audit report which raised questions about certain aspects of the TAO's management and that the contract with the TAO was only to be renewed on a temporary basis to ensure that corrective action was taken if necessary. The Commission would be monitoring the office's performance carefully and would review the position again before the end of the year. The Committee of Wise Men said later that Mr Santer's letter could 'only be qualified as misleading'.

Disillusionment

Obviously the rumours were growing and Mrs Waddington, deciding that it was better to be safe than sorry, asked the Commission for the report, although only after Leonardo II had already been voted on. Mrs Waddington never got a reply. She didn't need one in any case, because it was at that point that things started happening very fast.

On 5 November 1998 the European Parliament debated Leonardo II and voted in favour of the programme without having seen any of the conclusions from the Leonardo I audit. I was forced to look on helplessly from the public gallery while Parliament praised Mrs Cresson for the high standard of her programme. Parliament and Mrs Cresson agreed that this impressive programme should really be allocated a lot more money. Only two Green MEPs were critical, pointing out that Mrs Cresson needed to sort out the financial abuses that were evidently going on in the current Leonardo programme and that the Commission still had to answer Parliament's questions about the Leonardo audit.

It turned out later that the final report on the Leonardo audit had not been sent to Secretary-General Trojan and Commissioner Gradin until 4 November. The report was not passed on to DG XXII from DG XX until 6 November and Mrs Cresson saw it on 10 November. On 23 November the whole Commission received a copy.

However the version of the final report that was eventually sent to Parliament in December was punctuated with comments by DG XXII which played down the findings considerably. It was claimed that further investigation was needed; the assessment might not be accurate. The DG protested its complete innocence and as far as possible blamed everything on the TAO.

In the meantime, what was going on in UCLAF, the fraud

prevention unit? They had received the provisional report some time ago. What had the people in UCLAF done about it?

In the light of the report UCLAF had already concluded in an internal memo in September that the Leonardo TAO might have been guilty of sixteen criminal offences, four contract and accounting violations and two disciplinary violations. It unequivocally recommended legal action. However nothing was done until the following February. Eventually a member of the European Parliament became so irate about the whole affair that she took my evidence to the judicial authorities herself to have proceedings instituted. It was only after that that the Commission decided to refer a number of files to the authorities as well. The MEP was Nellie Maes, a member of the *Vlaamse Volksunie*. Was there really only one out of the 626 MEPs who understood what it was all about?

CHAPTER FIVE

Dirty Linen

It was not just Leonardo, either. In the past eighteen months I had come across a lot more peculiar things, some in Commission files and documents, some reported to me verbally by colleagues. Were these just rumours and gossip? If so they were very persistent. The press had had wind of all kinds of abuses for years. For a long time investigative journalists had been trying to get at the truth, but people in the Commission clammed up as soon as it came to evidence.

After the debacle over the Leonardo II vote in the European Parliament in November 1998, I realised that if every official remained loyal and only reported internally through the proper channels nothing would change.

Like Job among the ashes I sat brooding over a big pile of files of incriminating evidence. What should I do? My conscience was troubling me. Should I just stay with the organisation and stick to my duty of confidentiality—in other words keep quiet? Or should I follow my conscience and stand up for justice and the public interest? As far as I was concerned public confidence in Europe and in the future of European cooperation were in the public interest. It seemed arrogant to believe that I could do anything to change this. But if every Eurocrat thought like that and kept quiet, nothing would ever change. I decided to use the last avenue available to me in the Commission and go straight to the top.

In November I wrote a letter listing all the things that were wrong, not only in Leonardo but also elsewhere. I discussed it with colleagues and again they helped me by providing documents, including a report from Italy that had actually been sitting in a drawer for over a year. Some documents were sent to me anonymously. Colleagues also helped me to write the letter.

All the time I reminded myself that I did not need to come up with startling new revelations. It was better to show what had gone wrong up to now. In particular that meant analysing old cases and exposing their cause: the desire to keep dirty linen hidden at all costs, even if it meant that some abuses went unpunished.

By the end of November my letter had grown to 32 pages. I addressed it to the Dutch Secretary-General of the European Commission Carlo Trojan, marking it personal and confidential.

The letter contained the same information as the 34-page one I later sent to the European Parliament. The Leonardo and DG XXII affair was still the main focus. I was chiefly attacking the organisation's failure to take any action, despite all the evidence of irregularities and fraud.

In the letter I asked Trojan at least to send some of the existing reports to the Parliament so that it had the necessary information before it dealt with the Commission's discharge for 1996. The deadline for the submission of documents for this part-session was 4 December. So we only had a week, but that couldn't be helped. It was now or never. I decided to put paid to any doubt about my intentions by saying that if the Commission did not tell Parliament I was thinking of doing so myself.

Just before the weekend, on Friday 27 November 1998, I rang Trojan's secretary late in the afternoon.

'I'd like to make an appointment with Mr Trojan as soon as possible to hand over a letter to him'.

At first she fobbed me off, which was not unexpected. Obviously a man in his position was being pestered all day long by journalists and other people who wanted something from him. But when I explained to her what it was about, she conferred and made an appointment for me. And it was in the near future: I was to see Trojan straight after the weekend, at 8 a.m. on the Monday morning.

I had asked for this meeting against the advice of many of my colleagues. They did not think it would achieve much, but for one reason or another I was hoping to get a sympathetic hearing from Trojan. I had heard favourable reports of him. Anyway I had to give senior management one more chance to intervene at the last minute.

But the meeting that Monday morning was not a pleasant one. I gave Trojan the letter with a brief explanation. Trojan's immediate response was uncompromising. It was out of the question for me to send the information to the Parliament or the Court of Auditors myself. Obviously I must have looked at him a bit stupidly, because he thought he needed to explain it again. As Secretary-General of the Commission he might be appointed to chair the disciplinary board which would undoubtedly be set up. The board could decide to sack me.

Trojan did not treat the letter I had just handed him as personal and confidential. He wanted to pass it on to DG IX, DG XX and the fraud prevention unit.

So of course we were no further forward. I had sent countless letters to those departments and they had done nothing. In the meantime the European Parliament was simply being kept in the dark. I was also annoyed that he was going to send the note to Mrs Speculanti. In a section on the Joint Research Centre I had been fairly critical of my DG because audit reports from an audit in 1997 had been withheld. Trojan's unhelpful response put me in a particularly difficult position. Now there was really no going back.

On 1 December I wrote to the Commission President Mr Santer, the Commissioner for financial control and fraud prevention, Mrs Gradin, and the budget Commissioner, Mr Liikanen. I mentioned Trojan's reaction and reminded them of 4 December deadline for Parliament. I enclosed the letter I had handed over to Trojan. This time I also sent a copy to my legal adviser (the political secretary of my union, who was a lawyer).

Edith: 'Paul was gradually beginning to wonder whether anyone was bothering to read his file at all. Everyone just brushed him away as if he was an irritating little fly. The fact that he was a middle-ranking official seemed to be considered more relevant than what was in his letters. He was regularly called up before his director-general. Eventually, in November 1998, Paul plucked up his courage and made an appointment to see the Secretary-General, Mr Trojan. Again full of hopes of a sympathetic hearing, off he went, nervous about yet another meeting, to report the situation internally, as he was supposed to under the rules.

When he rang me later he was completely devastated. He had been given to understand that if he went on like this he could end up being sacked. I was very scared and begged Paul to give up his "crusade". I wouldn't do that now, but at the time I was still in awe of important people in influential positions. Paul must sometimes have asked himself then if he was really so crazy or if there was simply no one who had any sense of responsibility'.

Questions from Parliament

Now it was make or break time. President Santer had written to the President of the European Parliament on 9 October 1998 that he intended to give Article 206 of the European Treaty 'its full effect' in combating fraud. Under that article the Commission had to submit any necessary information to the European Parliament at Parliament's request. Therefore if Parliament specifically asked for certain documents the Commission had to comply. So the MEPs had to know which documents to ask for.

At the end of November I had a private meeting with Magda Aelvoet, chairman of the Green Group in the European Parliament. I explained the situation to her and said I was seriously considering passing on information to the Parliament. I thought I should warn MEPs of this. This seemed a better idea than suddenly presenting them with a letter full of important information and annexes just before the vote on the 1996 discharge. At the same time I wanted to be sure that they would do something about the letter, especially considering the enormous risk I would be taking.

It was a good meeting and not just in terms of the atmosphere. Mrs Aelvoet took the matter seriously and assured me that the letter—if I sent it, because I was still having doubts—would be given careful consideration. At any rate she could assure me that the Greens would take a strong stand.

The Greens did indeed act very quickly. When the European Parliament's Committee on Budgetary Control met a few days later, some (Green) MEPs asked again for a copy of the Leonardo I audit report. They insisted that they must have it in time for the start of the debate on the discharge for the 1996 budget. The Commission promised to provide a copy of the report as soon as it was ready. It was still in draft form and had not been approved.

The Commission never sent audit reports until there had been full consultation between the auditor and the department being audited.

In effect this was a refusal. In this particular case the Committee on Budgetary Control should certainly have seen the draft report, because the contents were extremely relevant to the vote on Leonardo II and the 1996 discharge.

> *Edith*: 'At the end of 1998 everything started happening at once. Paul told me he had to decide what to do with the information he had now collected. The European Parliament had to be told quickly about the abuses if it was to be able to do anything. It seemed quite logical to me that Paul should follow his conscience in this but I had no idea of the repercussions it would have. For Paul my eventual agreement was a confirmation, for me it was the answer to a question whose implications I did not really grasp'.

A Dilemma

Between 1 and 8 December I consulted a few colleagues who had helped in the past and advised me now on what to put in my letter. I spoke to people from the union, MEPs and European Parliament staff and took legal advice. Everyone stressed that I had to be certain of my facts. If I was, then I could back them up.

I discussed everything with Edith as well. She had already said several times that she would rather I let it drop, but in the end she conceded that if it meant so much to me I would just have to follow my conscience. I took this as a volte-face. Afterwards we had an argument about it.

Lastly I took the letter to one of the chaplains at the Holy

Trinity Anglican church, which I attended regularly on Sundays. Obviously the chaplain was not an accountant and he could not make an expert assessment of the contents, but I knew he could help me. I explained my dilemma. As a Christian I was still not sure whether I could and should go against the orders of my superiors. Also I was not certain that my motives were really so pure. We prayed together about it and he suggested the possible obstacles, circumstances or motives that might stand in the way of me sending the letter. He asked if I had spoken to my wife, whether there was anything in the staff regulations about this kind of thing and why I felt compelled to do it. I said I had been reading the Acts of the Apostles in the past few weeks and told him the ideas this had given me. I seemed to be feeling more and more strongly that now was the time to go ahead, even if I didn't think everything was settled yet. It seemed as though God always helped me when I was afraid.

Two days later, on 8 December, the chaplain told me he thought I could go ahead if I felt it was necessary. Obviously he could not take the decision for me, but he could not see that I had any ulterior motives. He thought it was an honest decision. I was terribly relieved, because I had already taken the decision myself a few hours earlier when I did not hear from him.

It was a last-minute decision. The next day I was actually going to do it. I spent the whole night revising the letter. I was running out of time and I couldn't find some of the annexes. I put a caveat on the letter that the annexes were confidential. I also blocked out the names of the people concerned who had not previously been mentioned in the press.

Edith: 'After deciding to go to the European Parliament, Paul worked through the night to finish the report as best as he could. It had to be the next morning, otherwise the decision to approve the Commission's expenditure could not actually be reversed and there would be little or no point in doing anything. He worked until he was completely worn out and the letters on his computer screen started to blur in front of his eyes. By early morning he couldn't carry on any longer and he had to stop whether he wanted to or not'.

D-day

On the morning of 9 December I took the letter to the Greens. I wanted them to make sure that the other political groups got it the same day. Magda Aelvoet promised me they would and she kept her promise. However the Greens had also called a press conference about the letter. I had no problem with that as such, but more copies had to be made for the press representatives. Before the letter was copied my name was hastily blocked out. But it was not done properly and my name leaked out to the press sooner than it should have done. The first phone calls came the very same day, a foretaste of what was to come.

The other political groups felt they had been discriminated against because they had only received the 34-page main report. The Greens had the 75 annexes totalling about 600 pages, but other MEPs could always come and look at these. I had insisted on that as an extra security precaution to protect the officials mentioned in the letter from the consequences. Some 'difficult' MEPs used that as an excuse to portray me as unreliable. The Socialists in particular were put out because they thought I had gone to the wrong political group. 'What were you thinking of, going to a small marginal group like the Greens?'

In any case the MEPs had relatively little interest in the matter. Only a few members were genuinely and openly interested in the contents of the letter and took the information seriously enough to ask me for further details. Apart from the Greens these included Nelly Maes (Vlaamse VU), Philippe De Coene (Vlaamse SP), Edward McMillan-Scott (British Conservative Party), Rosemarie Wemheuer (German SPD) and later in particular Michael Tappin (British Labour Party) and Jens-Peter Bonde (Danish June Movement).

It was a constant source of amazement to me, then and later, how the European Parliament exercised its control function. Whereas investigative journalists and parliamentary correspondents got to the bottom of the story over the next few months, I found it very difficult to persuade MEPs to read the letter. I sometimes felt that I had to do all the work for them, to carry out the investigation and even write the newspaper articles. Even in March I was asked by someone in Parliament to send them a copy of the letter, which by then had been widely publicised and was available on various Internet sites. I couldn't resist writing back that I hoped this MEP would do something with it (apart from just wiping his or her backside with it, but I didn't put that in).

The Court of Auditors

There was still another promise to be kept. I had told Trojan I would also report the situation to the European Court of Auditors. On Friday 11 December, two days after going to the Parliament, I rang the Court of Auditors to make an appointment with the President's cabinet.

Thinking about it later, the Court of Auditors exceeded all my expectations. After all that had happened I was wary of saying anything on the phone. But the response to my phone call was very gratifying, as if they had been waiting for my call. They were enthusiastic and concerned. I arranged with some of the staff on the phone that I would not only bring in the letter and its annexes, but also all the supporting documents.

There was a reason for that. In the letter I had said that incriminating files sometimes went missing at the Commission. If I was the only person who had a copy, all that was needed was a break-in at my home or office and everything could be hushed up. In that case I wouldn't have a leg to stand on. A few small incidents - including problems with my phone - had put me on my guard. In order to make some progress and for my own protection, I wanted to have copies of the documents at the Court of Auditors in Luxembourg. We arranged that I would turn up with the documents at 3 o'clock on the Monday afternoon, which would give me time to copy the most important documents in the morning.

But the following weekend turned out quite differently from what I had expected. The situation became threatening and I had several calls from colleagues warning me to be careful. Finally a reliable contact urged me to get out of my house and take all the files with me. I thought it was a bit strange, but in the end I followed the advice and went into hiding at a secret address that weekend with my mountain of papers. People in the European institutions were quickly beginning to divide into allies and sworn enemies and I didn't know who was in which camp.

On the Monday I arrived at the Court of Auditors with all my papers, much earlier than arranged. First of all I met Mr Welter, then the chef de cabinet, Mr Löhrer, and then the President, Professor Friedmann. They told me they appreciated what I had done and were interested in the contents of the files I had brought with me, of which I gave them a brief verbal explanation. For me this was enormously important. For the first time I heard European officials express genuine and unreserved appreciation of my action.

Everything was done very meticulously. A detailed receipt was made out, listing all the documents I left with them.

Edith: 'It seemed like a normal Sunday evening. Obviously Paul was feeling tense because he had to go to the Court of Auditors in Luxembourg the following day, but as far as I was concerned this tenseness was gradually becoming a permanent feature of our lives. Then came the first phone call from a colleague, saying that there were plans to sack him and Commissioner Liikanen had already taken the decision to start disciplinary proceedings but it was not to be announced until after the forthcoming vote in Parliament. Later that Sunday another call came through on his mobile. People were saying they really didn't think he should stay at home that night with all the files in his study. Paul left. What had we got ourselves into? It was a long and strange night, without any incidents. Paul got a good reception at the Court of Auditors. When he rang me he sounded elated. "Edith, they told me that I shouldn't worry too much about my future". That was the first of many statements that left us between hope and despair, but ultimately didn't give us any reassurance'.

An Historic Vote

On the evening before Parliament voted on the 1996 discharge the Commission sent the Parliament a sort of 'threatening letter'. The Commission argued that trust between the two institutions was essential if they were to function properly and the Commission had therefore complied with Parliament's earlier request to improve its financial management. The Commission was now halfway through the process and it would not be right to undermine the Commission's authority at the present stage. In other words, it would serve little purpose to refuse a discharge.

However, the Commission said, if Parliament did refuse a discharge it would have to carry it through to its logical conclusion and vote immediately for the dismissal of the whole Commission. The Commission did not believe that Parliament would have the nerve to do that.

The Socialist Group played along with the Commission. The Socialists announced a motion of no confidence so that they could announce later that they would be voting against their own motion and the Commission would remain firmly in office. Since the Socialist Group was the largest political group on Parliament, this was what should have happened. But then things got out of hand. A number of MEPs felt they had been blackmailed. The vote was an historic one. Parliament voted by 270 votes to 225 not to give a discharge for the Commission's 1996 annual accounts. This was a first in its history.

Christmas Holiday

Although I had already started my Christmas holiday, on 18 December, the day after the vote, I went into the office to look at a few files. I was going to do a bit more work at home over the holiday. I was bending over a drawer full of files when the phone rang. 'Paul van Buitenen speaking'. 'This is Schiff, in personnel. Can you come to DG IX?' 'Well actually I'm already on leave', I told him. 'I was going to go straight home again. What's it about?' 'I have to tell you that you're suspended, Mr van Buitenen'. 'Suspended?' So it was true. I felt a buzzing in my ears. What a wonderful Christmas present! And what was Edith going to say about it? I quickly pulled myself together. 'And can you tell me, Mr Schiff, on what grounds I am being suspended and what does it mean exactly?' 'If you come and see me I'll explain all the details'. I put my jacket on and went to see my colleagues and my boss. They told me Schiff had been trying to get hold of me all morning and had rung me at home as well. I realised that the Commission had actually waited deliberately until after Parliament had voted on the discharge, just as a colleague had predicted that hectic weekend when I took my files to the Court of Auditors.

I went rather nervously to personnel, expecting to see Mr Schiff, the head of unit. When I got there his secretary was the only person there. She told me Schiff did not wish to see me and I would be given a letter. She handed over the letter and I went into the corridor. I tore open the envelope and read the letter, which was in official-sounding language, in French naturally. It was true, I was suspended. Then, when I got to the last few lines, they took my breath away. I didn't know if I was seeing straight. Half my salary was being docked as well! I went back in and asked the secretary to explain, but she just fobbed me off. She couldn't tell me anything. I would have to see Mr Schiff about that and he really didn't have time to see me.

I was devastated. I thought for a moment of storming past the secretary into Schiff's office to ask him if that was normal, but I realised I had to stay calm and not make things worse. I felt angry, humiliated and depressed all at the same time. That was how a criminal must feel. In a daze I went back to my own building. I showed the letter to my colleagues. They reacted with surprise and disbelief. One of my colleagues began swearing and shouted at me that I shouldn't put up with it. I just laughed, thanked them and went home, totally empty, weary and defeated. I also had to explain it to Edith, but I didn't know what to tell her.

After a quick consultation with my lawyer, the following day I wrote a letter protesting against the decision to suspend me. When I thought about it, the fact that my salary was being halved whilst I was under suspension seemed to be the severest punishment possible. I also asked for a Dutch translation of the documents and a further explanation, because I still didn't understand what the suspension entailed. Was I merely suspended from my work, did I still have to turn up at the office, was I still allowed into EU premises? I have never had a reply.

Edith: 'Paul drove up in his Punto. He looked shaken. He had been suspended on half pay for disclosing information to unauthorised persons—the unauthorised persons being the members of the European Parliament.

Paul had honestly never expected such a severe punishment. I was mainly shocked and confused. It was like being attacked. I was presented with a fait accompli that I was not at all prepared for. We had been looking forward to a happy Christmas and a couple of days on a romantic trip together. Instead of which we had disciplinary proceedings and the threat of immediate dismissal hanging over our heads.

That evening we had planned a party game with the children in which everyone got a present if they answered a question correctly. The presents had already been wrapped and were under the Christmas tree. We decided to carry on as normal, for the sake of the children. I got a lovely vegetarian cookbook from Paul. We cooked something from it the next day and had an enjoyable afternoon. But the pain I had felt in my stomach whenever I thought of what was happening to us did not go away for several weeks. The romantic time we were going to spend together turned into weeks of arguments, reconciliations and anxiety about what was in store for us'.

The Court of Auditors at Work

Over the Christmas holiday I collected my files from the Court of Auditors in Luxembourg. Mr Welter, a member of the President's cabinet, and Mr Löhrer, the chef de cabinet, again gave me a friendly reception. They told me three copies had been made of the files and these were being kept in different places.

They were very frank. At the beginning, when the files were just sitting there, they were worried about them being taken. I must know that there were people in the Court of Auditors too who didn't like me. They showed me some recent correspondence between the President of the Court of Auditors and Mr Santer. Santer wrote to Professor Friedmann that he was not following the arrangements and practices that were customary between the Court of Auditors and the Commission. It had already been established in the first investigation that my information was misleading and partly inaccurate. Luckily Professor Friedmann did not let himself be swayed. He wrote back making it quite clear to Santer that the Court of Auditors was independent. It was for the Court to decide whether and how it received relevant documents. Friedmann said that Santer should not interfere in the business of the President of the European Court of Auditors. I was full of respect and admiration for the way Friedmann behaved.

Shortly after that I had a phone call that showed the care with which the Court of Auditors was treating me and how quickly they had gone to work on the files. A member of the Court's staff told me that UCLAF, the anti-fraud office, was coming to look at my files. Did I have any objections? I thought about it for a minute. In that strange weekend I had loaded quite a few items into my car, including a scribbling pad full of personal notes containing the names of my sources. I asked him to remove this. Otherwise everything could be used as far as I was concerned. The Court of Auditors promised to do that.

CHAPTER SIX

Letter to the European Parliament

I headed my letter to Magda Aelvoet, chairman of the Greens in the European Parliament, *'How the European Commission deals with its internal irregularities and fraud'*. Copies were sent to the chairmen of all the other political groups. In the introductory letter I explained that after countless attempts to go through official channels this letter was the only way left to me to expose the serious abuses going on in the Commission.

In view of the forthcoming 'discharge' (similar to approval of the annual accounts) for 1996 I considered it my duty to supply Parliament with information relevant to its decision, on the basis that Article 21 of the Staff Regulations allows an official to disregard the instructions of his superiors if criminal offences are involved.

I ended my introductory letter with the hope that MEPs would take the matter seriously and 'act with courage and strength in order to give a new impulse towards a more open cooperation between the European institutions'.

Finally I said that I had not sent the anonymous letter they had received a few weeks earlier and asked the MEPs to treat the annexes (75 in all) as confidential to protect my colleagues and the other people concerned.

I devoted a large part of the letter to the Leonardo affair, but

I also wrote about tourism, the Joint Research Centre, Commissioner Cresson, the Security Office and other issues.

Keeping Parliament Informed

I focused on information that could be of relevance for the European Parliament. I did not go into detail about the facts in the letter itself. These were clear from the annexes. After all my object was not to relay a juicy story about all the wheelings and dealings. I had written the letter to show that although the many irregularities in the Commission were known about and even well-documented too little was done about them after that. In all the cases I listed in the letter I explained what information was available but said that for various reasons it had been kept quiet.

In particular I reminded Parliament that it had the power to ask the Commission for documents and to insist on getting them. I gave examples of where Parliament had been successful in this and where it had not. Unfortunately most of the examples in the letter were cases in which Parliament had not been given the information it needed. Both the Commission and Parliament had been remiss. Sometimes earlier questions were repeated, but often the information was simply not supplied or, if it was, it was months or even years after Parliament had first asked for it. It was time for a change and a change was on its way. On 9 October 1998 President Santer had written to the President of the European Parliament that he intended to give Article 206 of the European Treaty 'its full effect' in combating fraud. Under that article the Commission had to submit any necessary information to the European Parliament at Parliament's request. Therefore, as Mrs Theato, the chairman of the Parliament's Committee on Budgets, rightly said, if the Committee asked for documents, it was not for the Commission to decide which documents to send. Parliament had to have access to all the documents that were relevant to the decision. In Mrs Theato's words 'the one being examined must not decide on what will be examined'. The Commission must not assume that the annual accounts would be approved automatically.

Tourism

The problems in the tourism sector were the earliest case in which the Commission's actions were open to question. The story began in 1989, when European Year of Tourism 1990 was launched. The idea behind the programme was that, with European cooperation on the increase, Europe's citizens needed to know more about each other's cultures. Tourism in Europe was the best way to achieve this. The programme was therefore set up to promote tourism, preferably the type of tourism in which people would actually learn something about other cultures and countries, but also tourism that gave people a respect for the environment, in other words ecological tourism.

The budget for the 1990 tourism programme was nearly £4 million. The total budget for the combined tourism programmes from 1989 to 1995 was nearly £25 million.

A specially created Tourism Unit in DG XXIII was responsible for the administration of the programme. Some of the work in the first year was contracted out, after a call for tenders, to a Technical Assistance Office or TAO, the firm Euroconseil. Organisations all over Europe could submit projects to implement the programme at local level. The projects were to be pre-selected in the Member States.

The Tourism Programme

In practice the subsidies for the innumerable projects were allocated more or less haphazardly. Recipients put forward projects unsolicited without any pre-selection, for instance after an invitation to submit projects. This applied to as many as half the projects between 1991 and 1992.

Often the rules were not followed when contracts were signed. There was cheating going on with the granting of subsidies, the use of funds and the accounting and budgetary rules. There was financial mismanagement and a lack of financial control: accounts not properly kept, incomplete files, belated notification, inefficient registration of mail. Invitations to tender and calls for the submission of proposals were not clear. The committees specially set up for that purpose, instead of being actively involved in the selection process, played a passive role and were merely kept informed of what was happening. There was no preselection in the Member States, or if there was it was not done correctly.

The Euroconseil TAO

Many contractors exploited the tourism programme. Euroconseil, the TAO running the programme, did particularly well out of it. It began with the call for tenders. This was not published in the Official Journal as it should have been. Of the firms invited to compete Euroconseil seemed to offer the best tender, but its rates were kept deliberately low. The technical capabilities and financial status of the tenderers were not evaluated. With such large contracts a bank guarantee normally has to be lodged, but that did not happen in this case.

In the first year everything appeared to go well with Euroconseil. After that various problems came to light. For instance the correspondents (a network in every Member State) were not paid. Euroconseil, with the agreement of DG XXIII, had used the money to increase the rates for experts. In 1990 an extra £160,000 or so was spent on setting up a new network of correspondents.

There was no supervision of Euroconseil consultants (records of attendance, for example). They often performed managerial duties that should have been undertaken by Commission officials. They were (too) involved in the selection and monitoring of projects. The inappropriate degree of responsibility allowed to Euroconseil was clear from the fact that it even answered written questions from the European Parliament. Not only that, they were critical questions about Euroconseil!

It soon transpired that Euroconseil had not really been the lowest bidder in the tender procedure. As soon as it came to the renewal of the contract the prices suddenly shot up, from approximately £130 a day under the first contract to £230 for the first renewal and after that £280! Euroconseil was also allowed to keep 20% of any money from sponsors, which could easily lead to conflicts of interest and in fact that proved to be the case. The first report by the Wise Men (Committee of Independent Experts), published in March 1999, gives a detailed account of what happened.

Euroconseil received unjustified payments totalling around £140,000, partly through transactions that could be regarded as fraudulent, as well as around £30,000 for the correspondents and £78,000 for work by a communications firm, who never received any of the money.

In the meantime Euroconseil went bankrupt. The Commission admitted to Parliament that there had been irregularities at the TAO. But in the final report there was no mention of the fact that it was actually fraud. Non-existent expenditure had been declared. Although this was earlier denied (in answer to a question from the Parliament), Euroconseil did in fact appear to have close links with a senior Parliament official.

Because of the Commission's inefficiency and delay in carrying out an internal investigation it has never been established whether an English director in DG XXIII and his French assistant played a discreditable role in the whole affair.

Projects

Many projects were subsidised in an ad hoc manner and were not really looked at properly. The last - and only really thorough - audit in 1998 revealed 236 incorrect payments. 193 payments totalling approximately £1.9 million were reclaimed; 24 recovery orders (for a total of £800,000) were being drawn up. In July 1998 all that had been repaid was about £350,000 from 61 recipients. There were numerous cases of fraudulent overpayment, involving 76 people and organisations. Criminal proceedings have now been instituted against some of these in Member States; other cases are still under investigation.

Ecological Tourism

In 1992 the European Parliament set aside a sum of £336,000 and upwards for an information network in Europe to promote ecological tourism. The firm selected, IPK, was to work with three partners. Of these, the Greek firm 01-Pliroforiki was allocated most of the work and the money. At the beginning of 1993, however, the Commission put pressure on IPK to accept a new partner, the German firm SFT. It is still not clear how that came about. Apparently the pressure was considerable. Because the Commission has been so inefficient and slow in setting up internal investigations it has never been established whether the German Director-General of DG XXIII was dishonestly involved. He was prematurely retired. At any rate the audit for 1993 showed that the contribution to IPK was only supposed to be in the region of £48,000, whereas about £190,000 had been paid at the beginning of 1993. It was not until 1997, when the case had been passed to the judicial authorities, that DG XXIII took the initiative in checking whether any of the money should be recovered and, if so, how much. The matter was then referred to the fraud prevention unit, UCLAF.

Two Leading Players

There were at least two key figures in the network of fraud and irregularities under the tourism programme.

The head of the tourism unit in DG XXIII did a great deal of outside work that was not in his job description. This led to embezzlement, corruption and favouritism. Without the knowledge of his senior management, he had interests in four different companies. He either managed them direct or transferred his share to his wife and mother-in-law. Two of the companies worked on EC programmes and were paid subsidies. He also improperly authorised quite large payments to at least four other contractors.

A conflict of interest also arose with a temporary employee in the unit and a detached national expert working on the programme in DG XXIII.

The temporary employee was involved in outside activities relating to tourism which were not authorised by the Commission and could be prejudicial to the EC work. He accepted airline tickets for his wife from an organisation he was working with. He also had direct contact with the organisation through his Commission work, which could lead to a conflict of interest.

After a lengthy investigation by various bodies from internal audit to the judicial authorities, which dragged on for just as long as the Leonardo investigation, the two of them were charged with fraud and corruption and prosecuted.

The head of unit was not sacked until 1995, but was allowed to keep his pension. The Belgian authorities were slightly harder on him; he was remanded in custody for a year.

The temporary employee was also sacked - and paid a severance allowance. He left with a total of around £60,000. The Committee of Independent Experts later took the view that in view of what had happened he was not entitled to the severance payment and he had been overpaid by over £30,000.

The Follow-up

My criticism of the follow-up to the tourism affair was mainly directed at the lengthy investigations that were still necessary when the fraud had already been identified at a very early stage (again through a whistleblower). I also criticised the handling of the case, with the two employees getting off very lightly. Even though one of them had to spend a year in a Belgian jail, neither was in any way held liable for the improperly paid subsidies, although the staff regulations do provide for that possibility. What is worse, important information was withheld from Parliament and the Commission did not cooperate fully with the Belgian judicial authorities.

Parliament had to ask questions for a third time about the handover of files to the judicial authorities in Belgium, France and Italy. MEPs were also unhappy about the supply of information and the time it took to deal with the case. As they pointed out in a motion, the Commission also had some responsibility for the cover-up of the two employees' crimes.

Much too long

Parliament had raised the alarm as far back as 1989. In its 1992 report the Court of Auditors drew attention to serious irregularities and improper payments bypassing all the normal procedures. In 1993 DG XX also found problems with the management of the tourism unit. The fraud prevention unit, UCLAF, was first brought in in 1994. In July 1993 an article appeared in a Greek newspaper accusing the head of the tourism unit of fraud and corruption. The article was brought to the attention of his senior management early in 1994. In 1994 the case was referred to the French and Belgian judicial authorities, as a result of which the head of unit was remanded in custody for a year.

The judicial authorities' enquiries were initially hampered by the Commission's refusal to waive the senior officials' immunity.

That was not the end of story. In November 1996 the Court of Auditors produced a special report on the Commission's tourism policy. In the light of its findings there was a further investigation, by Financial Control (DG XX), DG XXIII and UCLAF. There was more to come.

All this time attention had been focused mainly on two people, but they were not the only ones involved. There were whole files that had not been looked at in the various investigations and a couple of these were very interesting. There was a letter from the head of unit himself with very detailed information about irregularities committed by other DG XXIII staff, including very senior officials. A few MEPs were sent a copy. The document was found purely by chance two years later by two members of the special tourism audit team. However the 90 annexes went missing for a long time. I eventually got hold of them from a journalist. Also the judicial authorities did not get them from the Commission in the first place.

UCLAF and DG IX (personnel) never looked into the role of other officials. The Belgian authorities would have liked to but initially received no cooperation. In particular the top officials who might have been involved were protected and certain matters were never fully investigated. The Director-General of DG XXIII was retired prematurely. One director went to another department.

One thing is clear after the publication of the Wise Men's report in March 1999. I was wrong on a few details of the Tourism affair, but my letter to Parliament was for the most part perfectly correct.

The Security Office

The internal Security Office was responsible for the internal and external security of the Commission's buildings and staff. When necessary it also provided security staff for Commissioners and other officials. The Security Office was under the direct responsibility of the Commission President—initially Mr Delors, later Mr Santer—and his chef de cabinet. Several services, such as building security, were contracted out. In my letter to Parliament I touched on six points relating to the Security Office.

In 1992 the first whistleblower reported irregularities in the Security Office to the Delors cabinet. As a result an audit was conducted in 1993.

A second whistleblower went to the press in 1997, which led to the discovery of more serious administrative irregularities dating from 1992. This was in connection with the possibly fraudulent award of a security contract worth in the region of £50 million for the period 1992 to 1997.

People were given jobs in the Security Office without going through the proper procedures and favours were done for friends.

Staff in the Security Office had links with the far right in Belgium. I went into some detail about this in my letter to Parliament.

I also drew attention to the lack of control over the Security Office's position of power and the failure by the Commission's control departments to take any action.

Conclusions

After the publication of the Wise Men's report in March 1999 and the parliamentary hearings for the new Commissioners in the summer of 1999 I came to the following conclusions.

It appears from the answers to questions in the parliamentary hearings in August 1999 that Jacques Delors' chef de cabinet, who was responsible for the Security Office, received information as long ago as October 1992 which cast doubt on the tender procedure for the security contract. So this was not about the information that office supplies and furniture were going missing. That was also reported, but to another member of the cabinet, as the report states. I mentioned this confusion about the information that the Delors cabinet received in my letter to Parliament. The 1993 audit report did not recommend disciplinary proceedings; the recommendations that actually were made were acted upon. The only conclusion that can be drawn from the Wise Men's report is that disciplinary proceedings should have been started in 1993 in the light of the audit report.

Another investigation was started in 1997. What happened then illustrates how necessary whistleblowers are. Without the press coverage the serious irregularities in the tendering for this major security contract would never have come to light.

The staffing arrangements were chaotic. The Security Office took advantage of the contract with the security firm Group 4 to remedy its internal staff problems. Under the contract Group 4 provided 31 paid staff for the Security Office, DG XII, ECHO and EP1 for periods of up to a year and for non-security work. Many had been given jobs on the recommendation of senior officials, including the deputy director of the Security Office. Colleagues at the Commission were offered 'little favours' such as the cancellation of parking or drink-driving fines.

Although there were clear indications of links between the Security Office and people and organisations on the far right, the Wise Men's report paid very little attention to this issue, perhaps thinking that it was outside its terms of reference. In my letter to Parliament I pointed out that UCLAF's reporting was confined to financial irregularities. Consequently the shady connections between Security Office staff and right wing extremists in Belgium have never been fully investigated.

As regards the Security Office's position of power, the Wise Men's report concluded that ex-President Santer and his cabinet, who were strictly speaking responsible for the Office, never showed any interest in its operations. Because of this lack of supervision a 'state within a state' was allowed to develop.

The Committee did take a fairly positive view of the role of the control departments (UCLAF, Financial Control and DG IX discipline). My initial inference in the December letter that these departments were inefficient proved not to be correct in this case.

The Joint Research Centre (JRC)

A scandal blew up at the Joint Research Centre after a visit by a European Parliament delegation in 1998. According to press reports Parliament had uncovered six cases of favouritism, including a member of staff who had arranged lucrative contracts for his wife's firm, set up specially for the purpose. There were several instances where former members of staff who had started their own office had no difficulty in securing JRC contracts. UCLAF was called in. The European Parliament was gratified at the speedy response to the reported irregularities.

Not as Speedy as all That

Financial Control had already come across exactly the same

irregularities in the course of a routine audit in 1997. However the report had still not been released by November 1998 and had apparently not even been sent to UCLAF, let alone Parliament's Committee on Budgetary Control. It was even questionable whether this audit report would be brought into the new UCLAF investigation.

Again the impetus to investigate further came not from the internal control departments but from the European Parliament.

Although this case might seem fairly trivial, it played an important part in my decision to approach the European Parliament. I had already been hearing for some time from my colleagues that their audit reports were not taken seriously at the highest level in the Commission. This was an example. In my letter to Parliament I explained how my own Director-General in Financial Control was unwilling to approve the JRC audit report, for reasons that were not clear. When I later went to see the Secretary-General on 30 November 1998 and he told me he was not willing to treat my letter as personal or confidential and was going to pass it on to my Director-General, it obviously put me in a very awkward position. I knew exactly what my Director-General's reaction would be when she saw the letter and I realised at that point that there was no going back and I would actually have to take the matter to Parliament. That was eight months after I first said I was considering going to Parliament myself if necessary.

A Commissioner

That was what I entitled the section of my letter describing the activities of Mrs Cresson and her associates. In my eyes she had had one important virtue as a Commissioner: she managed to make her cabinet the most mobile in the Commission. She was less fortunate in her choice of staff. Many of them seemed to be involved in activities that were close to or even well beyond the pale. I happened to know about Commissioner Cresson because I had worked in a DG for which she was directly responsible, but I didn't know what the position was with other Commissioners.

Fraud and irregularities were uncovered in the Commission's special humanitarian aid section, ECHO, involving Mr Dony's offshore company and a Commission official, Mr Malpense. Mr Malpense was the father of a member of Mrs Cresson's cabinet. Dony's offshore company had to take on two people without any experience of humanitarian aid because they were friends of Malpense Jr. René Berthelot, a close friend of Mrs Cresson's, was also involved in another offshore company of Dony's. In fact Berthelot was offered the use of a flat by yet another company in Dony's network.

Two outside firms were involved in irregularities in the MED programme (which promoted cooperation with countries in the southern Mediterranean). One of the firms was run by contractors with whom Mrs Cresson's departments also had business dealings in other areas.

The shares in the Euroconseil TAO, which I mentioned earlier in connection with tourism, were partly owned by another company, Euro2C. The company was investigated by the judicial authorities in France. One of Mrs Cresson's cabinet staff was a senior consultant and representative of Euro2C. In a letter of recommendation this person was also named as the French correspondent of Euroconseil. The wife of the main shareholder in Euroconseil and Euro2C also worked for the two firms involved in the MED irregularities.

René Berthelot, who at some point shared the same residential address as Mrs Cresson, had secured medical research contracts through the Joint Research Centre and DG XII. According to recent audit reports their legitimacy was questionable. Mr

Berthelot's son was also given a contract in Mrs Cresson's departments.

Irregular contracts were awarded in various DGs through Mrs Cresson's 'communications unit'. The framework contracts for the communications unit were placed exclusively with firms in Brussels and Paris. I had already shown that one of these contracts had been awarded without going properly through the procedures. Various senior officials were involved. I reported the irregularities in 1997 but UCLAF was reluctant to investigate further.

The preparation and implementation of Mrs Cresson's White Paper on education and vocational training were full of irregularities. The administrative arrangements were in the hands of Mrs Cresson's cabinet and permanent advisers, including Professor Pneumann who was given several contracts.

In the Leonardo TAO affair there were indications that Mrs Cresson's cabinet was involved in the TAO's management. Mrs Cressons' departments opposed the cancellation of the TAO contract recommended by Financial Control. Her cabinet also interfered in the release and contents of the audit report drawing attention to the irregularities.

The structure that Mrs Cresson proposed for a new programme incorporating Leonardo II was the same as before, with a large outside Technical Assistance Office. Despite warnings the proposal—with a budget of £1.9 billion—was adopted.

I continued to list Mrs Cresson's associates, all involved in dubious activities.

I tried to show that it went much further than a few incidental and isolated instances of irregularity. From my own experiences in DG XXII I knew the cabinet interfered in day-to-day business and in a number of selection procedures. This all pointed to a management culture that has no place in a modern organisation.

My View Now

Looking back at my letter nine months later, I can see that I made some minor mistakes and that I was sometimes wide of the mark. That does not mean that I got the overall picture wrong. Things couldn't go on like that. I regularly heard people at work complaining that the results of audits were not taken seriously. What struck me was that the internal audit section in Financial Control was not properly appreciated. The way the fraud prevention unit worked left a lot to be desired. If I made mistakes it was because I did not have much time. I had to get the letter to Parliament by 9 December at the latest, otherwise there would not be time to consider it before the vote on the discharge of the budget on 17 December. A lot could have gone wrong with the letter. I realise that it was not the excellence of my letter that set the ball rolling. But fortunately all the work I had put in turned out not to have been wasted.

> *Edith:* 'This was an unfamiliar experience for me. I had to keep everything going at home as usual and go to work, which I found very exhausting. Paul was always there if I needed him, but otherwise he was living on his "fraud planet". I wanted his attention even when I didn't "need" him, just to spend an evening watching television with the children or doing some work in the garden without having to arrange it first. The borderline between work and home had disappeared. Not that I thought he was wrong to do it; it was hard to find fault with his campaign against serious abuses. But it upset me to see how home life was starting to take second place and how sometimes he did not realise that day-to-day family worries could be just as

worthwhile and important. And I had no idea of the impact Paul's detective work would have and how crucial it would turn out to be for Europe.

CHAPTER SEVEN

Going to the Press

I had done it—but without thinking about the consequences. These proved to be overwhelming. The suspension had been devastating, for both me and my family. What I had not anticipated was the enormous media interest. In the next few months we were almost overrun by the media. That had its good and its bad sides.

Looking back on it now, the pros outweighed the cons. For years investigative journalists had been digging to try and get at the truth behind the rumours and now for the first time they were openly supported by an insider. Although they had accumulated plenty of material, often they could not do much with it because they did not have access to the Commission or the system was too impenetrable for them. As far as they were concerned my action confirmed what they had long suspected. It was no longer just a sensational blown-up report that could well be untrue. They now had reliable corroboration from someone inside the organisation. It must have made them feel less helpless and besides that it gave an impetus to their work. Their perseverance was to be rewarded. They carried on asking 'awkward' questions and the integrity of the Europe institutions was one of the major stories of 1999.

Their persistence was also useful for me. They were my main

source of information now that I no longer heard anything from the Commission. Their dogged pursuit of the story over the next few months also kept attention focused on my own situation, the suspension and everything that followed it. Without the media I would have been destroyed.

Edith: 'On 9 December I had just got back from work and was looking forward to having a cup of coffee and reading the paper when the phone rang. It was my father. 'Edith, that wasn't Paul, was it, he didn't really do that? Go to the European Parliament with confidential information?' I was flabbergasted. How did my father know about it? He had read on Dutch teletext that an official had passed on documents about abuses in the Commission to the European Parliament. I was very alarmed and wondered how it had got on to teletext so quickly. Quickly turning the TV on, I said to my father. 'If it's on there, then I'm afraid it is Paul'. And there it was. As I was explaining to my father that it was not really as dramatic as it sounded, I wondered who I was trying to convince'.

I did not give any interviews immediately after the letter was published, or only very brief ones. I felt very uncertain and didn't really know what to do. After a few days the interest waned. Even after I was suspended on 18 December I did not contact the press. I was too devastated and I had to sort things out at home first. We had had a miserable Christmas, with rows and recriminations between Edith and me, after which we would make up and then it would start all over again. But as the Christmas holiday went on I began to realise that I was going to lose this battle if I kept quiet. I knew as soon as the new year started that I had to go to the press.

125

The First Interview

When I plucked up the courage to give my first interview I chose the paper myself. It was the Flemish daily *De Morgen*, which had a well known investigative journalist whose work I had always admired.

The interview was at *De Morgen's* editorial office on the morning of Sunday 3 January. Edith drove me there but said she would rather wait in the car. It was pouring with rain.

I went in feeling very nervous. I had already taken an enormous step in going to Parliament and I had no idea what this would lead to. Would it retrieve the situation or would I really be putting my job on the line? As I got out of the lift, I looked about me uncertainly. But as soon as I walked into the editorial office my curiosity got the better of me. It was a real newspaper office just like you see on TV, a big room with a jumble of desks and stacks of paper and newspapers all over the place. It wasn't busy that Sunday morning. People were working at computer screens or chatting. The atmosphere was very informal. They scarcely looked up as I walked by looking for a familiar face or someone who was expecting me. Some of them gave me a friendly nod. Eventually someone spoke to me and introduced themselves. Apparently they were expecting me, but the person I was supposed to see hadn't arrived yet. I asked how many people worked there and they told me this was the Sunday staff, a small team whose job it was to get the Monday paper out. Someone lent me his mug and they gave me a cup of coffee. I was beginning to feel at home. After I while I realised that Edith was going to have to wait longer than we thought and went outside to let her know. She decided to go on home. I would see if I could get a lift.

Luckily I had my briefcase with me, with a file in it that I had to return to someone. I asked if I could use the photocopier and as I was photocopying the person I was meeting came into the office. I finished the job and went in with hi. Another member of staff, Frans Steehhoudt, did the interview with me. It was that article that really started the ball rolling.

> *Edith*: 'It was pouring with rain that day. There is a market right by the *De Morgen* office every Sunday morning and I went there to kill time. It is a big weekly market, very lively, where you can buy absolutely anything. But it was cold and wet and there wasn't really anything I wanted so I went back to the car. After I had waited quite a while Paul tapped on the window and asked if I wanted to come up. I really didn't want to. This was still all very new to me and I didn't fancy sitting in a newspaper office while Paul gave an interview that was very important for him. I was afraid I would be in the way'.

The First Article

It was a major article that appeared in *De Morgen* the following morning, 4 January 1999. The headline was 'Eurocrat suspended after exposing fraud'. The following are a few extracts.

> *Paul van Buitenen, an official in DG XX, the European Commission's Financial Control department, has been given the severest possible punishment after sending the European Parliament (the EU body responsible for budgets) a long and well-documented report on how the Commission deals with frauds connected with contracts.*
>
> *His criticisms focus largely on European Commissioner Edith Cresson. Cresson alleges that Van Buitenen was previously sacked from her own education department for incompetence. van Buitenen says he was promoted. His ordeal started when he was transferred. 'On 1 January 1998 I was transferred at my own request from DG XXII, the Directorate-General responsible for vocational training programmes, to DG XX, which does financial audits of other DGs'.*

Van Buitenen's main aim was to draw attention to the mismanagement of the Leonardo da Vinci programme, a project with a total budget of over £400 million providing annual support for around 700 vocational training initiatives. van Buitenen and his colleagues claim that in many cases there were direct or indirect conflicts of interest in the allocations for the programme and the private partners were very lax about how the funds were spent. The day-to-day management of these programmes is contracted out to private firms, which win the lucrative contracts after an open call for tenders. In the case of the Leonardo programme the contract was awarded to a firm called Agenor NV, which was ultimately responsible for most of the budget.

Agenor was given nearly £6 million a year for operating expenses and could spend the remaining £400 million or so on projects.

A Flemish auditor found irregularities as far back as 1996, but they mainly came to light in 1997, when there was a more thorough inspection', says van Buitenen. 'That was what led me to get involved. Pressure was put on the auditor and his findings were disputed. It was an open secret in DG XXII that there was a cover-up. I started writing a personal report and looked at all the allegations. Quite a number of people volunteered information.'

In 1997 van Buitenen contacted UCLAF, the European Commission's fraud prevention unit. 'UCLAF can only make administrative enquiries. It has no investigating powers. If fraud cases are serious enough it has to pass the files on to the national judicial authorities. That didn't happen with my file, even though it was well-substantiated. They didn't even look into it'.

At van Buitenen's request DG XX, the department in which he was now working, started an investigation into his previous department, DG XXII. The report made it clear that there were indications of something wrong in the department.

It was only after DG XX had specifically asked for the report that things started to happen. In February 1998 it was decided at a meeting that DG XXII should be investigated, but only in relation to Agenor's part in the Leonardo da Vinci affair. The DG itself would not be investigated.

'My Director-General told me that I would not be allowed to do any more audits for this case. In other words I was supposed to stay in my office and not interview anyone else. On 26 March I wrote a long letter setting out my objections to the restrictions that had been placed on the investigation and the role of the fraud prevention unit. I drew attention to the role of Commissioner Cresson's cabinet and her departments. Lastly I threatened to inform the

European Parliament of the mismanagement. The letter, which was 20 pages long and had 40 annexes, was sent to all my senior management, including my Director-General. I also sent a copy to the director of UCLAF'.

... The official response to van Buitenen's letter came on 31 March. He was told he was being discharged from his responsibility to report abuses to his superiors since this evidently troubled his conscience.

On 5 and 6 May van Buitenen received two more letters rebuking him for talking to some of his former colleagues in DG XXII. He was told he was going against the instructions of his superiors, which was a breach of the Staff Regulations ....

On 17 July van Buitenen's allegations were borne out by the Leonardo investigation report. On 1 September he wrote to his Director-General saying that in spite of the decisions in the investigation nothing had changed. He was planning to inform the European Parliament. He repeated this on 28 October, but at a meeting with his Director-General he was forbidden to go to the Parliament, or the Court of Auditors which was interested in the case. A few days earlier, however, all the MEPs had been sent an anonymous letter exposing the malpractice. It was not van Buitenen who sent the letter, although many people believed that it was. It was not until 9 December that he sent a long letter with 75 annexes to Magda Aelvoet, chairman of the Greens, asking her to pass it on to the Parliament's Committee on Budgetary Control.

Five days after that van Buitenen found that he was barred from using part of the internal computer network. Four days later he was told he was to be suspended under Articles 12 and 17 of the Staff Regulations. It was alleged that by speaking out he had brought his office into disrepute and breached official secrecy. His salary was to be halved from 16 December while he was under investigation

DE MORGEN, 4 JANUARY 1999

A Victim?

The article had a tremendous impact. After it was published the whole thing really took off. Someone said to me later that it was that article that made all the difference. Suddenly there was a face to go with the story. Mine.

The media had been talking about the frauds and irregularities for years. Of course that annoyed the Commission, but it was not a serious problem for the Commissioners. Even when I gave my letter to the Greens in Parliament on 9 December it only led to the refusal of a discharge on 17 December 1998 and caused a minor stir. The Commission was still not really in any danger. It was not until 4 January 1999, when I came out with the story of how I had been suspended and my salary halved on 18 December 1998 that the picture changed. All of a sudden the media and the public had found a victim.

It was the press that launched the attack on the Commission. They did not pull their punches. Cresson and Marin were under fire and they fought back. Mrs Cresson gave champagne receptions for the press and protested her innocence. Earlier she had put it about that I was dismissed from her DG for incompetence, when in fact I had had been promoted before going to Financial Control of my own accord.

All sorts of rumours were flying around. For instance I was reported to have let journalists look at confidential files on the Security Office irregularities at my home. There was also a persistent allegation that I was an active member of Agalev, a Green party. It was true I belonged to the Greens, but I was certainly not an active member. That was brought up against me from time to time in the public debate, because it made it look as though I was letting my personal convictions interfere with my work.

So not only was I giving interviews explaining my letter, I was also having to refute the rumours. At home we kept an eye on the papers, the Internet and teletext for any news. I was sometimes disappointed at how ill-informed the journalists were. Apart from the seasoned European experts and investigative journalists, I had calls from reporters who had very little idea of what the whole thing was about and had not even bothered to read my letter. The worst were some of the articles in so-called quality papers. I had never spoken to the people who wrote them but they did not let the facts stand in the way of a good story. However other articles restored my hopes that something would come out of it.

In the same edition in which my interview appeared, *De Morgen* also published an article with the headline "Calls to sack Cresson and Marin". The following are a few extracts:

Renate Schmidt, vice-chairman of the German Social Democrats, has called for the dismissal of the Spanish European Commissioner Manuel Marin and his French colleague Edith Cresson. Schmidt says that they should accept political responsibility for the corruption, favouritism and fraud in their departments. At the plenary sitting in Strasbourg she called on MEPs and fellow party members to remove the Commission from office through a motion of no confidence tabled by the Socialists. In mid-December the European Parliament refused to give the Commission a discharge for the 1996 budget because of a series of corruption and fraud scandals. It was mainly the Christian Democrats, the smaller left wing parties and the Greens that voted against the discharge.

Earlier the Commission had threatened that if the Parliament would not give a discharge it would then have to table a motion of no confidence right away.

The Socialist Group, the majority of whose members had voted for the discharge, went along with this so that those who had refused the discharge would follow suit. At the same time Pauline Green, chairman of the Socialist Group, announced that her group would vote against the motion. The thinking behind this was that a two-thirds majority was needed for the motion to be carried and the Commission would therefore end up with a vote of confidence. Before Christmas, MEP Ingo Friedrich, a Bavarian CSU member, had asked Chancellor Gerhard Schröder to start dismissal proceedings against Marin and Cresson.

Under the EU Treaty the Council or the Commission can apply to the Court of Justice for the compulsory retirement of any member of the Commission who no longer fulfils the conditions required for the performance of his duties or has been guilty of serious misconduct

DE MORGEN, *4 JANUARY 1999*

131

Edith: 'Paul kept saying that it was all going to take off in January. After our lonely Christmas I wondered what could possibly happen. I had felt so isolated in the weeks before that that it didn't seem likely that anything would change in January. But a couple of days after Paul's *De Morgen* interview there was a phone call from BBC Radio asking if he would do an interview for the Breakfast Show.

Paul was right. It really did take off from then on. When I got home from work on the Wednesday the road and our driveway were so full of press and TV vans and cars that I had trouble parking. I could see glaring camera lights through the windows. I thought I might be able to get in through the garage and the kitchen without being seen. The stomach ache came back with a vengeance. What were all these people doing in our living room? I felt like crawling under a large stone, but I steeled myself and walked in to the kitchen, I quickly closed the living room door and thought I was safe. Then Paul came dashing into the kitchen and asked me to take his mobile and the other phone. The phone had to be unplugged when he was filming because it kept ringing and interfering with the recording.

There was a clear pattern to the next few days. I went to work and then came home to answer the phone and make a note of all the phone calls. I pulled the curtains in the kitchen to avoid being seen or filmed from the living room. Sometimes I rushed in and took Paul something to eat. We were so overwhelmed by the interest that we were afraid to say that sometimes Paul needed to eat too. I spent hours shut up in the kitchen. Every day our drive, our living room and our garden were full of media people from all over Europe, while I worried about Paul and the children and what was going to happen next'.

The Press Gets Moving

The standard of reporting was variable, as far I was able to judge. There were inaccuracies, some due to ignorance and some from sources that wanted to discredit me. For instance an article by Remco de Jong that appeared in *Het Parool* on 5 January quoted a Commissioner as saying I had used forged documents. Evidently the Commission was expecting this argument to exonerate it so that it would not have to go into the contents of my letter. The article contained a few more interesting points:

EU SUSPENDS DUTCH OFFICIAL FOR FRAUD LEAK

... In particular van Buitenen made a number of allegations against French Commissioner Edith Cresson, saying that she had fixed friends up with jobs for which they were very highly paid and were required to do very little in return.

Cresson brought a libel suit against the French newspaper Libération which published earlier revelations.

At the December part-session the Socialist Group in the European Parliament tabled a motion of no confidence against the whole Commission, hoping it would be rejected and that in this way Parliament would indirectly express its confidence in the Commission.
The Socialists were in favour of a discharge, feeling that the Commission had taken some steps towards tackling fraud effectively. The motion of no confidence will almost certainly be rejected because the Christian Democrats, who were against the discharge, are not prepared to dismiss the Commission. It is unprecedented for Parliament to vote the Commission out of office.
According to van Buitenen the Commission does not take fraud control seriously. He felt it his duty 'as a Christian' to inform the Parliament of his findings. The Commission has suspended him for a breach of official secrecy. A spokesman alleged yesterday that some of the documents van Buitenen was using are forged. It is also alleged that van Buitenen has been transferred

several times in the past few years for poor performance, which he denies.

HET PAROOL, 5 JANUARY 1999

The sting was in the tail ... My letter was obviously not about Mrs Cresson's favouritism. It focused on the incompetent handling of internal fraud and irregularities in the Commission. It just happened that in the cases I knew about a lot of Cresson's colleagues were involved in irregularities. These cases were just examples as far as I was concerned.

The role of the Socialist Group was interesting and complicated. The group could express confidence in the Commission through a motion of no confidence because the Socialists had more than a third of the votes in the European Parliament. Since a motion of no confidence needed a two-thirds majority, the group could defeat a motion of no confidence on its own, at least if all the Socialists toed the group line and followed the group chairman's voting advice. This was by no means a foregone conclusion because the German Socialists, especially the budgetary control spokesman Rosemarie Wemhauer, were much more critical of the Commission than many of their fellow members from other countries.

Against their better judgment the Socialists were satisfied with the improvements in the Commission's fraud policy. It was no secret in the Parliament that the Commission's recent proposals to set up an independent body, OLAF, to replace the internal UCLAF were totally inadequate. The independence was just a front. The proposals the Commission had put forward in early December were not serious; it was simply playing for time.

I later read in *Het Nieuwsblad/De Gentenaar* at the beginning of January what the official Commission line on me was:

The European official who exposed cases of fraud at the end of last year has been suspended by the EU, allegedly for spreading lies.

EU spokesman Martine Reicherts confirmed reports of the suspension yesterday. She said the main reason the Dutch official had been suspended was not that he allowed a file to be leaked but that he told 'lies' in it. There was no indication yesterday what these lies were.

HET NIEUWSBLAD/DE GENTENAAR

In typical *Telegraaf* style, *Telegraaf* journalist Ruud Kreutzer condensed my interview into a few pithy statements, which gave me quite a shock when I read them later:

'If they can't keep me quiet that means the end of the present culture of secrecy in Brussels. But this is only the tip of the iceberg. I would be delighted if I could be given unlimited powers to investigate all the rumours that are going round. Maybe there are too few people who are ready to stick their necks out. Colleagues tell each other all kinds of stories over coffee about wheeling and dealing by Commissioners and cheating by officials, but it's just talk. Nobody ever does anything about it', says van Buitenen.

DE TELEGRAAF, 5 JANUARY 1999

The complaints by other political groups in the European Parliament that they had been missed out reached the ears of the press. It was quite untrue. On the day I took the letter to the Greens I sent copies to all the other political groups. I did hear later that there were problems in getting hold of the 75 annexes. The other political groups did not get them, but they could always look at the copies the Greens had. The other groups saw it as a political ploy by the Greens. But the Greens were not trying to monopolise the letter; I asked them myself to treat the annexes as confidential. I couldn't really see what the other groups were complaining about, because I found that a lot of MEPs didn't even read the letter.

The *Brabants Nieuwsblad/De Stem* took a special interest in me because I came from that part of the country. On 5 January it reported:

Yesterday the Commission circulated a background document on Van Buitenen, referred to in the document as 'Mr X'. The European official has incensed the Commission by handing over files that are under investigation by the judicial authorities or internally to the Greens in the European Parliament. Van Buitenen had previously tried unsuccessfully to report the irregularities he came across as an auditor to top officials and Commissioners.

That paper was also one of the first to start campaigning for me to be exonerated. Journalists took the initiative in trying to track down the people who were really responsible straightaway. In the same article on 5 January they also cross-examined Christian Democrat MEPs Hanja Maij-Weggen and Piet Dankert and Commissioner Van Miert:

CDA MEP Hanja Maij-Weggen wants to get rid of two European Commissioners, Edith Cresson and Vice-President Manuel Marin. The President of the Commission can start proceedings himself at the Court of Justice. But Maij-Weggen wants the European Parliament's budgets committee, which is in possession of the mass of papers leaked by van Buitenen, to investigate all the allegations first. 'The Commission has to refute the allegations. If it can't do that, it's in big trouble'.

She defends van Buitenen. He might have breached confidentiality but he was clearly facing a moral dilemma. 'It's quite possible that serious misconduct was actually hushed up and he cannot reconcile that with his conscience'.

Piet Dankert, a Social Democrat member of the Committee on Budgetary Control, gave the Commission the benefit of the doubt last month in the debate on the approval of the Commission's 1996 annual accounts. Now he is having second thoughts. Things are not looking good for the Commission, in his view. Its reputation is in ruins. But he does not think that heads should roll. Van Buitenen provides no hard evidence of fraud and corruption. However, says Dankert, the documents he has given us do indicate a need for further investigation. He thinks it is a shame the Commission is not helping to scotch the rumours.

On Monday the Belgian Commissioner, Mr Van Miert, strongly denied a cover-up by the Commission. But he admitted that the institution is not properly equipped to deal with this kind of problem. 'We are being asked to do the impossible. The Commission cannot take action against officials itself when there is no evidence of corruption or abuse of power'. Van Buitenen, on the other hand, thinks that even suspicions of misconduct should be reported to the police. It doesn't often come to that. But the people who expose the scandals like van Buitenen have more to fear.

BRABANTS NIEUWSBLAD/DE STEM, 5 JANUARY 1999

The last sentence is all too true. The paper asked me for my comments. When I was asked whether I saw myself as a latter-day Don Quixote tilting at windmills, I replied:

'I have asked myself that question over and over again in the past few weeks. Looking at it coolly and dispassionately, I have to say that I have bitten off more than I can chew. But I still feel that what I am doing is worth it. I just underestimated the forces the Commission would bring into play against some-one who discloses information ... I have a wife and two sons, aged 14 and 15. If I had known what would happen to me before I started, I would not have done it.'

BRABANTS NIEUWSBLAD/DE STEM, 5 JANUARY 1999

Happy New Year

President Santer's famous press conference was held on Wednesday 6 January 1999. Commissioner Liikanen also took part. Santer emphasised that it was a new year's conference and boasted of the Commission's achievements over the past year. The room was full of journalists from here, there and every-where. They had obviously come not for Santer's new year's greetings but for what he euphemistically referred to in his opening speech as 'the news'. He and later Commissioner Liikanen were grilled about the fraud, irregularities and favouritism and personally challenged on alleged conflicts of interest, in particular the preferential treatment allegedly given to their wives. They dismissed the suggestion with a smile, Liikanen arguing that in his country men and women were equal and it was quite normal for a wife to have her own career. He completely ignored the point of the question, which was whether his wife was getting contracts from the Commission. 'What about if I show you a contract signed by your wife?', the journalist threatened. Very wisely Liikanen did not rise to the bait.

It turned out later that the organisation for which his wife worked had in fact had six contracts with the Commission worth nearly £1 million, all signed after Liikanen became Commissioner. A very nice independent career!

The first questions about the repercussions for me also came up at the press conference. The Commissioners insisted that I was the one who was at fault and my suspension was entirely justified. They also said that the problems I had drawn attention to were nothing new. Commission spokesman Martine Reicherts said that these frauds were already being investigated in the Commission and in some cases by the legal authorities as well. The Commission said that my letter had hampered the investigation.

Volkskrant correspondent Geert-Jan Bogaerts reported on the press conference the following day:

> Santer and Liikanen have a simple message: all the recent allegations of fraud, corruption and favouritism are either made up or are being thoroughly investigated, in some cases by the legal authorities as well.
>
> 'It's a witch hunt', Dutch Commission representative Hans van den Broek said later. 'With 17,000 employees, hundreds of programmes, and billions of expenditure, it is inevitable that something will occasionally go wrong. It is important to sort out the problems as quickly as possible. But it's gone too far now. The current climate is endangering the credibility of the whole Commission'.
>
> Santer defended himself against allegations which until then had only come up in a little-known paper in his home country of Luxembourg. It was reported that Santer's wife had interests in a property company that rented buildings to the Commission. The Commission was late in launching its counter-attack.

Next week the European Parliament is to debate a motion of no confidence. Santer will only go if the motion gets the necessary two-thirds majority. He does not believe that a simple majority will harm his political position.

The President was slightly more convincing when he defended the decision to suspend a Dutch official who had leaked the fraud documents. Yesterday he revealed the whistleblower's name for the first time. Now it was Paul van Buitenen and not Mr X any longer. The Commission had even made up a complete file on him, which was available from Santer's spokesman's office. Van Buitenen was a troublemaker; the problems he reported were already under investigation and there was nothing new. He had been warned that going to the Parliament could cost him his job.

'I entirely agree', Van den Broek said. 'Even senior Commission officials took the time to listen to him. That's unusual for officials in his grade. If you tolerate this kind of thing you can create a precedent if you're not careful. But we're going to have to put up with the bad image it's given us for a while'.

Immediately after the press conference the phone calls came pouring in. I had calls from the BBC, ARD, Canal+, RTL 1, Libre Belgique, Danish TV, Deutsche Welle, Reuters, Stern, ZDF, BBC World and various MEPs

DE VOLKSKRANT, 7 JANUARY 1999

After the press conference André Riche made the situation quite clear in the Belgian daily *Le Soir.*

'The suspension of an official who talked too much has unleashed a storm. Has the Commission made a fatal mistake? Yesterday the Commission was harsh in its criticism of the European official suspended for passing on documents to the European Parliament. It tried to play down the revelations, but it seems this is only beginning of the story.'

LE SOIR, 7 JANUARY 1999

Overrun by the Media

After the press conference we were approached by all kinds of TV programmes wanting to come and film or have me as a guest on chat shows. Hordes of TV vans turned up in our village.

139

There was no end to it. The journalists wanted to involve the whole family. Poor Edith didn't know which way to turn …

Edith: Bart Nijpels from *Netwerk* wanted to film Paul at home with his family. I said doubtfully that Paul was very tired and I didn't think there was anything interesting here to film. Bart Nijpels answered, 'I just want to film the people behind the story. We'll do it very nicely'. He was very kind and persuasive, but I got terribly nervous at the thought of a television team being with us for several days, in our own home. I didn't want to interrupt Paul for too long because he had already given interviews to four television teams, three magazines, two newspapers and one radio programme that day and was still talking to a lot of people in the living room, but after quite a bit of discussion I decided to say yes.

Netwerk wanted to come and take pictures that evening so that they could be shown the following Sunday evening. I felt just like a character in a comedy film as I went on with my daily chores: is the house clean and tidy, does my hair look OK, what am I going to say? Bart Nijpels had been very persuasive on the phone, but now I had agreed I started to get very nervous. I really didn't want to be filmed! I was tired and I had been looking forward to a normal weekend after such an exhausting and chaotic week. But I did it anyway, because I knew Paul needed the publicity if he was going to come out of this unscathed.

Luckily Bart Nijpels was good at dealing with inexperienced TV performers. He arrived with a bunch of flowers and quickly put us at our ease. The cameraman and sound engineer turned out not to be ogres either. They weren't trying to pry into our private lives behind our backs. As I put the flowers in a vase they were already film-ing and I felt very uncomfortable. After they had finished the following day, I asked Bart Nijpels anxiously, "You won't leave it in if I have said anything silly that might hurt Paul?" I was very worried about that afterwards. He assured me it was all going to be OK. The programme, the first of three, was all about Paul and it was very good. Luckily they left me and the children out of it. I was grate-ful to them for that'.

CHAPTER EIGHT

Outside Support

Now the fighting had really broken out and the arena had moved to the media. It was a peculiar situation that was to last for several months. In one way I was isolated, but at the same time people were talking publicly about what I had done and what was happening to me and even complete strangers were for or against me. To my relief I had supporters standing up for me in the press right at the start. *De Volkskrant*, for instance, published the following article under the headline 'Suspended for no reason?'

> *Hein Verkerk, spokesman for the European Parliament's Greens, says it is quite wrong … In suspending van Buitenen the Commission is being extraordinarily intimidating. There is only one reason for the suspension: the Commission is scared stiff that misconduct will be exposed. Article 17 of its Staff Regulations forbids the disclosure of information to anyone unauthorised. That is what van Buitenen is accused of. But Article 21 of the Regulations requires him to breach confidentiality if crime is involved and Van Buitenen is relying on that article to justify his actions. There was no one he could pass the information on to. He was called up in front of Carlo Trojan, the Commission's Secretary-General and most senior official, and told that if he did pass it on he would be sacked. Trojan denies having said that*

> *DE VOLKSKRANT, 6 JANUARY 1999*

As *De Volkskrant* so rightly says: It is the old story: the messenger is attacked instead of the people who are actually responsible for the irregularities and fraud. The article continues with comments from various sources:

> Labour MEP Piet Dankert: 'Van Buitenen not only went to the European Parliament about the fraud, he also went to the press. He gave a press conference. It does not seem to me that the Commission was exceeding its authority. The documents van Buitenen has produced are not all that convincing. There is very little proof and a lot of it is already known about. We are going to find out now what's going on, what are the new facts he is reporting and we shall be looking into them'.
>
> J. van Herpen, national administrator, Abvakabo civil service union, Zoetermeer: 'I heard on the news on Monday evening that the official has contravened two articles in the Staff Regulations. I don't know what the regulations are in Brussels. I wouldn't have thought van Buitenen did anything wrong in handing the documents over to the European Parliament. If that isn't the controlling body for the European Union, then what is?'
>
> Dr. Christe, lawyer and legal expert for De Volkskrant: 'Officials have an obligation to be loyal and respect confidentiality. An official can be suspended for serious breaches of those obligations. But they can also be abused. It would not be the first time an official has been suspended because he knows too much about corruption. The conscientious whistleblower is an easy target in any organisation that has something to hide'

> DE VOLKSKRANT, 6 JANUARY 1999

In *De Telegraaf* on 7 January columnist Rob Hoogland asked in his inimitable fashion how on earth the Commission came to suspend me on the grounds that I had passed my files on to unauthorised persons. The unauthorised persons then turned out to be the European Parliament. To make quite sure he had got his facts straight he had to check that Brussels is actually in Europe and not in the People's Republic of China, where things like that are not unexpected. Luckily I was still able to laugh when I read that. Thank goodness we had not yet sunk that low in Brussels.

Spin-off

The press seized on the cases I had drawn attention to in my letter and were now keeping a vigilant eye on developments. On 6
January *De Morgen* reported that MEP Nelly Maes was taking
the Leonardo case to the Belgian judicial authorities. She lodged
a complaint with the Brussels public prosecutor's office. After she
and her assistant Bart Staes had looked through my letter they
decided that when there were such clear indications of misuse of
Community funds Maes had a duty as an MEP to request a judicial investigation. To be honest I was pleased about that from a
personal point of view too because it backed up my reliance on
Article 21 of the Staff Regulations. By doing this she confirmed
that crimes might actually have been committed. She was one of
the few MEPs who acted as a true representative of the people.

I was forced to stay at home but I didn't have to miss anything. Everything was now out in the open. On 8 January the
Brabants Nieuwsblad/De Stem reported on Santer's approach to
the European Court of Auditors:

> In a letter to the President of the European Court of Auditors, Commission
> President Jacques Santer complained about the action by Dutch EU official
> Paul van Buitenen and the way in which this 'junior official' had been received
> by the top person in the Court of Auditors.
>
> Van Buitenen came to Luxembourg with a car full of files and told the
> Court of Auditors about his investigation into irregularities and alleged fraud
> at the Commission. The Court of Auditors, the independent control body which
> investigates the Commission's implementation programmes, is not afraid to give
> the Brussels institutions a rap over the knuckles.
>
> Yesterday a Commission spokesman denied interference in the Court of
> Auditors' affairs. She said that Santer had simply explained that van Buitenen
> had come by this information unlawfully and it should not be circulated. The
> Court's President, Bernhard Friedmann, replied that he had acted according to
> the rules. On Wednesday the Commission distributed details of all the initia-
> tives it had taken since 1995 to ensure more efficient management. This

lengthy process does not stop fraud and malpractice because the EU's structure is so complex. If the Commission does eventually report fraud or corruption it proves impossible for investigators to find their way through the EU maze. Not having sufficient specialist knowledge or manpower they are unable to get anywhere with their investigation The same thing happened with the European Year of Tourism subsidies in 1990. The people involved were sacked, but the loose ends were never tied up. It is debatable in fact whether Belgian criminal law is actually applicable to foreign EU officials working in Brussels

BRABANTS NIEUWSBLAD/DE STEM, 8 JANUARY 1999

The Story of the Guns

The story of the Security Office's sniper rifles appeared in the press at the same time. The Commission blundered on that occasion; they had used one of my letters, in which I referred to guns, to make out I had a persecution complex. It was reported in the British press, including the Daily Telegraph, that according to a Commission spokesman the claim that rifles had been purchased was investigated and turned out to be completely unfounded. Bodyguards were allowed to carry hand guns but the allegation about the rifles was 'absolutely crazy'.

On 8 January I had a phone call from one of my colleagues saying he could let me have proof to the contrary. I was delighted, because I had actually seen an order form for the guns but had never been able to get hold of a copy. He got me a copy of the 1992 order form for two heavy duty rifles with support, sights and two silencers (normally used by gangsters and assassins) plus four hand guns the very next day. He also urged me to keep up the fight. 'Go screw them, Paul!'

On Saturday 9 January it was reported in the papers (including *The Guardian*) that Commission spokesman Thierry Daman was now admitting the internal security service had two sniper rifles and two machine rifles, although it had earlier been denied.

What is interesting about this is not whether the Security

Office should or should not have had the guns. It is symptomatic of the Commission's whole attitude. First of all it refuses to admit that it simply knows nothing about these embarrassing situations, then it makes confident public statements that are only withdrawn when they are proved to be wrong. The Commission gradually destroyed its own credibility. The press, of course, pounced on the story:

> *Apparently wild allegations from Mr van Buitenen, that the Commission possessed sniper rifles with telescopic lenses and silencers, were first denied. Last week, however, the Commission admitted that they had the weapons - although they still deny suggestions that Mr van Buitenen was intimidated.*

> THE INDEPENDENT, 12 JANUARY 1999

> *As the new year kicked off, Commissioners themselves personally handed out copies of a letter van Buitenen had written to his superiors in the institution in which he warned that security guards were obtaining rifles complete with telescopic lenses and silencers; proof, they said, that the man was deranged. There were red faces all round when it turned out that rifles had indeed been procured, even though the institution said this was for genuine reasons of security*

> EUROPEAN VOICE, 27 JANUARY 1999

Pandemonium

While I was under suspension I worked harder than ever. Every day I was having to deal with media people from all over Europe. One day there was even a Japanese journalist! Our relatives often couldn't get through to us because the phone was permanently engaged. But my mother and in-laws did not give up. They followed every development closely and stood by us through thick and thin.

At the same time I was working my way through the files. There was so much I still hadn't read. Colleagues and informants had given me stacks of documents and the information kept coming in. Now I had gone public with the information quite a few colleagues in the Commission plucked up courage and sent me evidence of other malpractice, sometimes anonymously. Sometimes, though, I felt as though they had left me to carry the can. I could take all the risks for them; they would not stick their necks out themselves. For a while there was talk about another official who was also on the point of disclosing information. High level negotiations were going on with intermediaries, but in the end he backed out. Everybody was afraid of what could happen to whistleblowers.

I was pleasantly surprised when on 8 March I read a full-page article in *De Morgen* about Mrs Cresson's White Paper and the irregularities involving Professor Pneumann. It was the first in a series of four articles before the publication of the Wise Men's report. I was impressed. The articles were sharp and well-written, the facts complete and accurate. I heard on the grapevine that the articles had created quite a stir in DG XXII.

Edith: 'I sat at the kitchen table with two phones in front of me. They never stopped ringing. We were caught up in a whirl of activity and we had no idea what was coming next. The family couldn't phone us, it was impossible to get through. They read in the papers or saw on television what the Commissioners were saying about Paul and how they were making him out to be untrustworthy and unreliable. The only thing I could do to let my feelings out between phone calls was to write poetry:

> When they ask me
> "What's it like for you?"
> I say to myself
> Somehow we'll cope
> And see it through.

But then the silence
Alone it seems so tall
Everywhere I look
Appears a growing wall'.

The Vote of No Confidence

The European Parliament was to debate the matter on 14
January. It would also be voting on the vote of no confidence
tabled by the Socialists, who were taking it for granted that it
would not get the necessary two-thirds majority.

Edith and I went to the European Parliament that day, wondering what the outcome would be. We were met by Clive
Firstbond, an adviser working at the Parliament. First of all he
showed us round the building. We were overwhelmed, and even
more so by his comments about the struggle I still had in front
of me. He suggested that it would either break me, in which case
I would end up ruined, or I would come out of it well and be
snapped up for important work. That certainly didn't make me
feel any happier when I had already put up such a fight. It made
me uneasy, especially since Edith was again realising how uncertain our situation was.

We followed the voting on the internal video system in the
office of a Swedish Green MEP in the Parliament building, with
Clive explaining the votes to us. The MEPs told their fellow
group members how to vote with a thumbs up or thumbs down
signal.

In all the commotion they even talked about my position in
the Parliament - and that would not be the last time. To my surprise the Liberals, Greens and Christian Democrats had tabled a
motion asking Santer to come to an amicable settlement with
me. I saw Mrs Green, the leader of the Socialists, make a thumbs

down signal. The motion was not carried. There were 238 votes in favour, 286 against and 16 abstentions. Even so the 238 votes in favour were encouraging; I needed all the moral support I could get at that point.

Mrs Green had played for high stakes. The vote of no confidence she had tabled as a matter of form was not carried, but the vote did show that Parliament was not unanimously behind the Commission. As many as 42% of MEPs supported the vote of no confidence, which was not all that sound a backing for the Commission.

The following day the *Algemeen Dagblad* commented:

> *The Socialist Group, the dominant group with its 214 members, followed that blunder with another : a vote of no confidence which, even though it was not carried, significantly weakened the position of the mainly Socialist Commission.*

ALGEMEEN DAGBLAD, 15 JANUARY 1999

After refusing the 1996 discharge the European Parliament had shown its teeth for the second time. The following day the papers were full of it. *De Morgen* quoted the Parliament's triumphant President: 'The balance of power in Europe has shifted from the Commission to the Parliament'. But in the same article *De Morgen* also criticised the European Parliament:

> *Even so the 626 MEPs did not entirely come up smelling of roses. As it turned out they were not well informed and authoritative enough to make the Commissioners aware of their responsibility. A typical example was the pathetic performance in the Committee on Social Affairs, with Commissioner Cresson only having to ward off very superficial questions about the possible misappropriation of funds. There was never any real debate, mainly because the MEPs did not have a sound enough grasp of the facts.*

DE MORGEN, 15 JANUARY 1999

Mrs Cresson did not fare so well at the meeting of the Committee on Budgetary Control on 23 February. British Labour MEP Michael Tappin showed that even Socialists could be critical. Much to the displeasure of his political group leader, Pauline Green, he ended his impassioned and well-argued speech with a call for Mrs Cresson's resignation. Michael Tappin was one of the few to show a bit of backbone.

Independent Experts

One outcome of the debate was that a Committee of Wise Men was to be set up to assess the situation and give a totally independent opinion. This looked suspiciously like one of the Commission's notorious delaying tactics: 'we are investigating the matter'. On the other hand the committee was given a very strict deadline. The 'Wise Men' had fewer than two months to examine the facts and were to submit a report to Parliament by 15 March.

I hoped the committee would be genuinely independent. It would be a surprise ...

The press had its doubts too, especially about Parliament passing the buck:

> ... So an outside committee of experts is to do the dirty work. Quite a few (Flemish) MEPs would have preferred to see a proper parliamentary committee of enquiry set up, but had to admit that they didn't have the time to sit on it. Whether the eight (sic) independent experts will have the time, seeing that they have to complete their report by the end of March, remains to be seen.
>
> DE MORGEN, 15 JANUARY 1999

Commissioners Under Fire

When Parliament sat on 14 January a vote of no confidence was also tabled against the two Commissioners who seemed to have the most to worry about. To my mind the motion against Cresson and Marin was unfair because the responsibility actually lay with the whole Commission. After all the whole Commission had tolerated their behaviour for a long time. There was little doubt that other Commissioners were also responsible for dishonesty in their departments. As far as I was concerned it was pure chance that the Cresson and Marin examples happened to be the ones that came to light. Even though the motion was not carried it did give out a strong political signal:

> *Marin ... could still be safe. Edith Cresson's position is less secure. She might have survived the last few days but she has not done herself any favours. If the 'committee of wise men' studies the fraud files a bit more carefully than the MEPs this is merely a stay of execution.*
>
> DE MORGEN, 15 JANUARY 1999

> *The bearded Spaniard, who has squandered millions of European taxpayers' money and has by his own admission made a lot of mistakes over the past 14 years, is to be allowed to keep up the good work. Europe has survived its most serious institutional crisis so far. While one Commissioner reports back on his mobile that he will be staying on for a while after all, a couple of MEPs man-fully cut their their losses. They can console themselves with the thought that a very significant minority (42%) no longer has any confidence in the Commission and there will be a further debate in March. Pat Cox, leader of the European Liberal Democrats, says that as far as they are concerned this Commission is finished politically.*
>
> ALGEMEEN DAGBLAD, 15 JANUARY 1999

More Evidence

While Parliament was sitting I suddenly received a phone call. I was told that Mr Trovato, the Acting Director-General of DG XXII, who was staying in Strasbourg at the time, had had reports that large quantities of documents were being destroyed in the Leonardo TAO. He phoned DG XXII in Brussels straightaway and told Lejeffe to look into it, which he did. Even the rubbish containers outside the TAO were searched, but nothing was found.

At home I worked through the stacks of new files, some of which cast new light on the Perry Lux case. I was finding out more and more. What I had touched on in my letter was in many cases just the tip of the iceberg. For instance I received copies of contracts with a Finnish government organisation that Mrs Liikanen worked for. The organisation had managed to land quite a few contracts with the Commission since her husband became Commissioner. She had even signed one as chairman of the organisation and she was also the project manager. Nothing wrong with that in itself, but it did make you think.

A journalist gave me the 90 pages of the missing file in the tourism case, the notes by the convicted head of unit on what other officials in his DG were up to. He told me that the Belgian judicial authorities had also ordered him to hand over a copy for the criminal investigation. This suggested that the authorities had not managed to get the file from the Commission. I wondered whether UCLAF had the file and what they had done with it.

Support

When I called on a senior colleague, he assured me very seriously of his support. 'Paul, although we can't say it openly, you should know that we're all behind you'.

Although he felt that my approach was a bit drastic and I didn't always separate the main issues from the side issues, he did think it was high time something was done about the irregularities that were in danger of becoming generally accepted in the Commission. I would have preferred it if officials had expressed their support openly, but it was always good to have backing from someone who knew what it was all about.

Edith: 'One evening one of Paul's friends and "sources" turned up to hand over some documents. She rattled on in her rapid French, telling me I mustn't worry. "Paul's going to win, I'm sure of that, in ten months you'll see, Paul will win!"

My heart nearly stopped. Ten months! It had not even been going on for a month yet and I was feeling at the end of my tether!

A lady rang from the Netherlands who had heard about Paul on the TV and had phoned up immediately. She rang me every week from then on and sent me a beautiful poem. She would not give her address because she didn't want any thanks. She was one of the many who wrote, phoned or even said they would pray for us. These people kept us going'.

We got letters and cards from strangers which were very heartening. People e-mailed us to pledge their support. We even got an e-mail offering us a refuge in Hong Kong!

Edith: 'It was very hard to be cheerful and enthusiastic at work in spite of everything that kept going through my head. Luckily most people were very sympathetic. One of my pupils said to me, "I've heard about your husband, I think it's terrible what they're doing to him. When I heard it on the radio it made my flesh creep". People like her helped me more than they could know. Other people's sympathy made the situation easier to bear and less frightening for me'.

At the end of January the two of us were in Düsseldorf. I had been giving a talk there. Afterwards we went for a meal in a nearby brewery pub where there was a carnival atmosphere. It was the day before the traditional 'women's day' festival. We got into conversation with a lady butcher and her family and they warned me not to wear a tie the next day because it might be cut off!

> *Edith*: You're allowed to do that on women's day. The women cut off everyone's ties and the men get a kiss in return. Most of the men were wearing special ties and were quite happy to have them cut off!
>
> I wanted to take back something nice for my parents and mother-in-law for looking after the boys, so the butcher took us to her shop at 11 o'clock at night for us to buy some home-made Düsseldorf black pudding. And because she admired Paul for bringing the European scandals out into the open ("Is that really you?"), she presented us with four garlic sausages for the journey as well. I didn't have the heart to tell her we were vegetarians ... Encounters like that always gave us fresh heart'.

Media Attention

When we were going to bed we had to unplug the phone because it never stopped ringing. At the end of January Edith and I went to Germany for a couple of days to record a chat show. At the time life was completely hectic. In the morning we had a whole Swedish television team in the house and they moved all the furniture around to get the right shot. In the afternoon we were picked up by the German chauffeur.

> *Edith*: 'There was very heavy security at the studio, we had to go past a lot of people with earphones and nervous expressions. We soon found out why. One of the other

guests on the chat show was an Italian lawyer who was fighting against the Mafia. We saw from the opening film how she could not take a step outside her door unless she was surrounded by five heavily armed carabinieri. Her predecessor had been murdered by the mafia. Paul told me later that it had made a big impression on him. He realised there were people who were doing a lot more to fight injustice'.

Those few weeks were taken up with 'media training'. I was made up, I learned about pre-programme briefings and found out that I sometimes had to say the same thing four times over in front of the camera. I also realised that it's best to let things take their course and not try and plan everything in advance if it is to come across as spontaneous on the screen. All you need to do is tell the truth. I did sometimes find it difficult to express myself when the interview was in a foreign language. In the Netherlands and Germany people often went for a drink or a meal after the transmission and carried on discussing the programme.

> *Edith*: 'When we were driven home the next morning I said to Paul as we reached the Belgian border. "I feel as if we are going back into enemy territory". And it really was like that. We were going back into the arena. The telephone never stopped ringing. Every day I followed the news in the papers, on TV and on teletext. The news was full of the Commissioners venting their fury on Paul. I clenched my teeth when I saw them making him out to be a "troublemaker" and an "unimportant junior official"'.

TV journalists seemed to think that women and cooking went together. Mrs Cresson artfully played along with this by being filmed cooking a meal, at the same time light-heartedly dismissing all the allegations. Even in our home Edith was not safe in the kitchen. One day a BBC camera crew was there filming her while she worked.

Edith: 'I wanted to do everything I could to help Paul so I let them all come into the kitchen, although I really couldn't see what was interesting about a housewife doing the cooking. It soon started to get on my nerves having a camera and a bright light over my shoulder following everything I did. The pans were simmering with the lids on and everything was ready. After a couple of minutes the cameraman gestured at the biggest pan and asked, "Could you just stir it a bit?". Ruefully I took the lid off the pan and pointed at the cauliflower. There was not much to stir'.

The Judicial Investigation

The tourism and Security Office cases were already in the hands of the Belgian legal authorities. Thanks to MEP Nelly Maes a new judicial investigation was starting into the Leonardo case. The Brussels examining magistrate, Mr Beukmans, took up the case from February onwards. The senior Agenor and Leonardo managers had already gone in January. *De Morgen* reported:

> *The two top people in Agenor, chairman XXX and director XXX, resigned last month of their own accord*

> DE MORGEN, 8 FEBRUARY 1999

The same article contrasted the judicial investigation with the work of the Committee of Wise Men, which had just got under way. *De Morgen's* view was that a judicial investigation was at least clear. What was going to happen with the Wise Men's opinion was still very much in the air.

> *The problem is that the experts cannot make any enquiries or investigate any facts that are already being looked at in a national judicial investigation. According to UCL professor Joe Verhoeven, who provides legal advice at the request of the European Parliament's Greens, the committee of experts has no legal basis in either the EU treaty or EU law. Commission officials wanting to help the committee in its work will have to do so on a voluntary basis. Verhoeven warns that if they assist the committee they have no right to protection against any official action.*
>
> DE MORGEN, *8 FEBRUARY 1999*

I was assuming that both the Committee of Wise Men and the examining magistrate would be wanting to interview me at some point, but before making a statement I had to get authority from the Commission. I would have to apply to Santer for my immunity to be waived.

One of my informants at the Leonardo TAO was also interviewed by the examining magistrate and phoned me nervously to ask for copies of any files that might back up his statement. I discussed with him whether it might not be better for the examining magistrate to get the stuff straight from me. However, it was complicated. Until I had been discharged from my duty of confidentiality and could be interviewed by the magistrate I could not hand over any files to him. If I did they would be unlawfully obtained evidence. So I had to get my immunity waived quickly because I knew the files were important for the judicial investigation.

At the same time I realised that the Commission had probably only sent a very limited selection of material to the authorities. I knew from my informants that someone in UCLAF had assured Agenor that the file sent to the authorities contained no indications of fraud. Could that really be true? Might it not be a convenient way of reassuring Agenor and was all that information really going to be left out of the file? I could scarcely believe it, it was just like a thriller. Later on I actually got it in writing. And this was when the indications of fraud at the Leonardo TAO were so clear ... and UCLAF knew about them too!

I made an appointment with my union lawyer to go through the cases properly. When I went into the building the security people asked if I had an appointment with my lawyer and I was allowed through. That was the only Commission building I was allowed into, but only because my lawyer had his office there.

My lawyer told me that the case was probably being investigated by the same examining magistrate as the Security Office case, which he thought would be an advantage.

We drew up a letter to Santer asking for me to be exempted from the official secrecy obligation for the Belgian investigation. In the letter I took the opportunity to remind Santer that I wanted my job as an auditor in DG XX back. I was after all qualified for the job. If they were thinking of transferring me, then I would only consider a job in an auditing and investigating body such as the European Court of Auditors, the European Parliament's Committee on Budgetary Control or OLAF (the independent successor to UCLAF).

Finally my lawyer urged me to keep my distance from particular political parties around 15 March when the Wise Men's report was due to come out. Many of the Parliament's political groups would probably hold press conferences. It would be better for my case if I did not get involved in the political arguments, unless the parliamentary base was broad enough. I had to avoid giving the impression that I was politically involved.

The interview by the Committee of Wise Men lasted a whole

evening. From eight o'clock to nearly midnight four of the five committee members and their assistants fired question after question at me. I had taken my lawyer with me, but the interview turned out better than I expected. On the whole the questions were very much to the point. At the end of the meeting I handed over a few more documents, including information on various commissioners.

Edith: 'Paul and I were quite convinced that now we were getting near 15 March, the day the Committee of Wise Men was to publish its report, we would soon see an end to our uncertainty. Everyone was assuming that what happened to Paul depended on the conclusions of the report. That made the situation a bit more bearable for me. I could fix on a date. After that there might be some prospect of a decision on Paul's suspension and disciplinary proceedings.

At the beginning of March we finally got a bit of peace. There were still phone calls from journalists, but far fewer. People made comments like, "Don't you miss all the attention now?" Paul and I looked at each other as if to say, "Is it you that's crazy or is it us?" How could anyone think that you would miss such constant disruption in your home and private life?'

CHAPTER NINE

The Wise Men's Report

As 15 March approached the tension rose. What would the Committee come up with? Would its report be a cover-up? I had been totally honest with the Wise Men, telling them everything I knew and providing them with the written information from which they had to draw their own conclusions. But what would they do with it?

Once again the phone was ringing non-stop, but I had nothing new to tell the journalists. All we could do was wait for the report; everything else was pure speculation. We were just hanging on. Luckily we had something to take our minds off things. On 14 March Edith and I went to Cologne, where Edith Müller, a Green MEP on the Budgetary Control committee, wanted to interview me in front of an audience.

> *Edith*: 'I always liked going with Paul when he was giving a talk somewhere. It also helped me to understand the situation. You sensed people's outrage when they heard about the abuses in the Commission and especially the way Paul was being punished for sending the letter to the European Parliament. I could feel their warmth and sympathy and on the return journey in the train both Paul and I were particularly conscious of how isolated his position was.

Though of course I realised that only he could really know what it felt like'.

I was working on my laptop in the German hotel room. The TV was on in the background—it was good for my German—and Edith was lying on the bed reading a newspaper. We looked at each other and at that moment it came to me what an empty way of life it was, being on your own and staying in one hotel after another. 'Imagine if I got a job like this and had to go on business trips all the time'. Edith looked on the bright side. 'I'll just go with you as often as I can'.

On the television they were talking about a German army unit which had recruited a lot of foreign and naturalised soldiers, mostly from Poland, Turkey and Yugoslavia. The report was encouraging; apparently everyone was accepted as a German soldier and there were very few problems. I liked the idea of that. It was how things should be.

When we were on the train home the mobile began ringing constantly again. Things had started moving in Brussels. People were saying that the commissioners involved had been allowed to see the parts of the report referring specifically to them the evening before. Excited journalists were ringing from Brussels to say that there was a lot of coming and going at the Breydel building where the commissioners had their offices. Some journalists had managed to speak to the drivers.

It was all very hectic because the European elections were also imminent. All the political groups were keeping an eye on each other and looking for a strategy that would give them the maximum electoral advantage. The Greens wanted to hold a press conference immediately after the Wise Men's report appeared. They were anxious for me to take part, but I remembered my lawyer's advice not to get mixed up in the political arguments. That would just be playing into the hands of the Socialists' leader, Pauline Green. She had already been putting it about that the whole thing was just an election stunt by the Greens and that I was on a Green list. I did not commit myself, although I was a member of the Flemish Green party, Agalev, and I thought that the Greens were the only group whose behaviour on the fraud issue had always been above reproach.

I would only agree to take part if there was a press conference covering a broad political spectrum. That seemed unlikely to happen, but eventually two MEPs with very different political views, the German Green MEP Edith Müller and the British Conservative Edward McMillan-Scott, took the initiative and arranged a joint press conference. I thought that was a broad enough spectrum for me to speak to the press in Parliament.

Edith: 'There was wild speculation about who, what and where. 15 March was an anxious day for Paul. Would he be rehabilitated when the report confirmed his observations? Would he be able to go back to work in financial control without delay and, above all, would the disciplinary pro-ceedings be dropped? The Netwerk film crew followed Paul again that day. Once again the house was in total pan-demonium. Journalists from all over Europe wanted to know where Paul was when the report was published'.

The Report

On Monday 15 March everyone was kept in suspense for quite a while longer. I didn't leave for the European Parliament until midday. Journalists and MEPs and crowds of other people were milling about the building. Speculation was rife but the report had not arrived yet. It was not distributed until 5 o'clock that afternoon. Various political groups asked me to go through the report with them. I went and sat with the Greens.

The press conference was due to begin at seven and we only had until then to look at the report. I started reading and was amazed.

The report was clearer and more forceful than I had dared to hope. It gave a concise outline of the irregularities that had been identified, the Commission's way of dealing with them and the Wise Men's view of this. The verdict was damning. I would not have dared to put it so strongly myself, but then I was not an authority. The wording was sharp and unequivocal. The Committee was also honest enough to admit when it had too little information to be able to make a judgment. The experts said that they had come across a number of further cases which they had not yet had time to investigate. I immediately thought to myself that I would love to be involved when they did.

In general, though, I could see that the Wise Men had really gone into the subject thoroughly. They had completed an enormous task, interviewed everyone in the space of about six weeks, read most of the documents and even written a masterly short report.

They had come to the conclusion that the Commission was not doing enough about obvious misconduct. Either it was not investigated at all or, if it was, the investigation was too slow or incomplete. Instances went unpunished and any punishments that were imposed were remarkably lenient. This was not new to me, but I was amazingly relieved to see it confirmed so precisely and accurately. One particular sentence in the Wise Men's concluding remarks caused a considerable stir: 'It is becoming difficult to find anyone who has even the slightest sense of responsibility'.

Putting it in football terms, I might have made a reasonably good pass, but the Wise Men had slammed the ball into the net.

The report was published immediately and also appeared on the Internet in various European languages. Only a few days later it was reported in the press that a million people had visited the European Parliament website on which the report appeared. On the Monday the server became overloaded and extra sites had to be opened to cope with the demand.

Edith: 'He rang me straightaway. "At any rate the report is clear and firm. Really tough. Mrs Cresson is singled out. Her position is untenable now. It's not just nepotism but also the fact that the Commission could have acted on various cases years ago. You've no need to worry any longer, everything's going to work out fine"'.

The Press Conference

I went off to the press conference with the Netwerk camera crew on my heels. At the conference I told the press: 'I am a genuine whistleblower. From my point of view the importance of today's report is not that it corroborates the allegations I made on 9 December. It is important because for a long time there have been signs that things are wrong in our organisation and now they are finally being properly investigated.'

I explained how I had tried to deal with the situation through the normal official channels and how in the end I was forced to expose the facts through Parliament. I asked them to spare a thought for the predicament I was in, suspended on half-pay for the past three months. That was what happened to whistleblowers.

I concluded by saying that I had often felt very isolated and I wanted to thank those who had supported me in this difficult period, colleagues, journalists and MEPs as well as my family and friends.

Then they started firing questions at me. I needed to watch what I said and had prepared myself carefully.

Do you want to become an MEP?

'If I did I would be on a list'.

Do you think Mrs Cresson should resign?

'As an official it's not for me to decide. That is up to the Parliament'.

The report confirms the letter you sent last year. Are you pleased about that?

'My aim in sending the letter was to press for a full investigation, which the Commission had been putting off for over a year. I am certainly glad that has happened. But this report is only an interim step reminding the Commission of its responsibilities. That was not the aim of my letter at the time'.

The Member States want to set up a new fraud prevention unit, OLAF, but OLAF will be developed from UCLAF. What do you feel about that?

'The European institutions really need an independent fraud prevention unit which has the capacity to start investigations. UCLAF is not independent. It seems to me more logical for the fraud prevention unit to come under the European Court of Auditors, which is able to guarantee the necessary independence'.

Edith: 'He was enormously relieved and so was I. It seemed that the months of uncertainty were over. The report's conclusions about the way the Commission worked were damning. "It is becoming difficult to find anyone who has even the slightest sense of responsibility".

Paul was interviewed live outside the Parliament building, spoke to a lot more people and finally arrived home absolutely exhausted, still with a camera crew in tow. At home we all had something to drink and speculated about what this would mean for Europe. Which commissioners would be resigning and what would the consequences be?'

The Fall of the Commission

Late in the evening I was gradually starting to unwind. Now we had to wait and see what would happen at the special parliamentary sitting in a week's time. The European Parliament would be debating the Wise Men's conclusions in detail and would add its own conclusions.

That night one of our visitors had a call on his mobile from journalists who were still in Brussels. At 1 o'clock in the morning we heard to our amazement that the whole Commission had resigned. Everyone in the house was elated, but Edith and I were more bewildered and shocked. It was astonishing that this was the indirect result of my action in December.

Over the next few days it was pandemonium again. The public response was enormous and people were just assuming that I could now return to work with no trouble at all.

Everyone was congratulating me, but why? It had never been my aim to start a political row and bring about the downfall of the Commission. I just wanted to show that things were wrong in the Commission and that something should be done about them.

Edith: 'At one point an Austrian TV reporter asked Paul, "Has David slain Goliath?" "No", Paul answered laconically, "Goliath has slain himself". Things were getting out of hand again. Now and then I had the feeling that we were all playing parts in a film. One day an enormous outside broadcast van with a dish aerial on it turned up for a TV transmission. It couldn't park outside our door because it would block the whole street. In the end it had to turn into the driveway in a neighbour's front garden. A lot of people from the neighbourhood came and looked on curiously and we were afraid to show our faces outside. Big side poles were pulled out from the van to make a firm base for the 30 metre high mast. Later on the neighbour told me he had to give his personal details so that his roof could be insured for one hour. Massive cables were hauled around and people were going backwards and forwards between our front door and the living room to get everything ready for the filming. There were bright lights everywhere and our cat shot out into the darkness in a panic. It looked as though they were going to spend a week making a full-length film, but barely half an hour later they started dismantling everything again. After all that Paul spoke for three minutes live on the Belgian news programme *Ter Zake'*.

Media Comment

The media were full of the story. I read the articles carefully. They seemed to go into the Wise Men's report in much more detail than my letter. In view of the direct consequences it had had that was not altogether surprising.

The *Algemeen Dagblad* described the report as 'disastrous for the European Commission' and quoted the Wise Men's comment on the 'loss of control by the political authorities over the Administration that they are supposedly running'. For this, according to the Wise Men, both individual commissioners and the Commission as a whole bore a heavy responsibility.

De Morgen's comments were highly critical:

> *The European Commission must go. The Socialist Group and most of the opposition in the European Parliament are calling for its immediate dismissal.*

The European Parliament will force the Commission to stand down next week if it does not resign of its own accord. The Commission's survival was looking doubtful even while it was still considering its position. But after the damning report completed yesterday by the Committee of Wise Men the Parliament has very little choice. In the Committee's view the EU's management is a mess. Fraud and mismanagement have been able to take root because the Commission has no control over its administration.

Yesterday afternoon the Committee put a bomb under the Commission with this harsh judgment. MEPs immediately called for its collective dismissal but at that stage it was still not clear whether the Socialists, the largest political group with well over 200 members, would be unanimous. A few hours later it turned out that they were.

According to the Wise Men the problems are not confined to individual commissioners like the French Socialist Edith Cresson (research) or her Spanish colleague Manuel Marin (Mediterranean policy). They are more far-reaching; it is the whole culture that is at fault. The Commission did not know what was happening under its responsibility or it deliberately let things slide. Three commissioners (Cresson, Wulf-Mathies and Pinheiro) were guilty of favouritism. Either they did nothing about fraud and irregularities (Cresson and Marin) or they were unaware of them (Bonino).

So the European Commission has, with a very bad grace, resigned. You can even have a certain amount of sympathy with the bitter comments by some of the commissioners. In essence the activities that forced the Commission to commit collective hara-kiri were relatively minor and no doubt quite a few of the commissioners have done their jobs well and conscientiously. But even so they must bear some of the responsibility. Because the Commission refused to pay enough attention to what was going on, consistently passed the buck and treated the media and the European Parliament so arrogantly, the Committee of Wise Men eventually came to the damning but accurate conclusion that it was almost impossible to find anyone willing to accept responsibility. If the Commission had heeded damaging reports and information from the start, if it had told its officials to carry out proper audits instead of suspending them when they raised the alarm, if, in short, it had responded as it should have done, then it would not be in the fix it is now.

DE MORGEN, 17 MARCH 1999

Commissioners Furious

The Commission's resignation was not in itself cause for rejoicing. Quite the contrary. The timing could not have been worse. The Commission still had nine months to go before it was due to bow out, in which time it was supposed to take a number of important decisions, particularly on Agenda 2000 which outlined future EU policy and financing. The European elections were also imminent and the situation was not likely to have done much for the European Union's credibility. In the same period the press reported various scandals in the European Parliament, such as MEPs who never turned up but still claimed their attendance allowances. In fact it was a real tragedy.

In the meantime the outgoing commissioners were furious at their more or less enforced resignation. The ones who had been accused were protesting their innocence and the others were claiming they were being victimised for their colleagues' misconduct – or even mine. And still no one was responsible.

Mrs Cresson used every means at her disposal to defend herself in the press. Once again everything was in the public arena and the battle was being fought in the media:

> ... Edith Cresson maintains that the Wise Men's report in which she was so heavily criticised was a frame-up. Cresson told the French newspaper Le Figaro on Wednesday that the report published on Monday evening was rewritten at the last moment. 'Someone is trying to give the impression that I knew all along that some things were not working and that I misled the European Parliament'. She says she knows for certain that changes were made to the report on Monday which she did not see when she first read it on Sunday.
>
> In another interview with the French newspaper Le Parisien, Cresson accuses the Germans. 'German Conservatives who have it in for the Socialist commissioners are making out that the Commission is irresponsible with money'.
>
> Cresson says that her resignation also shows the gulf between the northern and southern Member States. 'No one from the south was involved in this

witch-hunt'.

Frenchman Pierre Lelong, one of the five members of the Committee of Wise Men, confirmed yesterday evening that amendments were made to the report between Sunday and Monday, but they were 'very minor'. 'Eleven commissioners came to see us between 2 and 7.30 p.m. on Sunday so that they could make any last-minute comments and we drew up the final text that night. The final amendments were incorporated then', says Lelong. 'The only changes that were made were very minor and did not affect the general conclusions'.

DE MORGEN, *18 MARCH 1999*

None of the commissioners was willing to resign. They gave vent to their feelings in the international media and emotions were high. I was surprised at the strength of their reactions and I wondered if the journalists were exaggerating the situation:

Insulted, humiliated and deeply wounded, the 20 commissioners are furious that they will not be allowed to serve out their last year of office.

'It's a disgrace', says President Santer tremulously. 'And I shall say that as long as I am sitting here.' Which will not be for much longer, because a single sentence in the 135-page report by the Committee of Wise Men, which took six weeks to investigate the Commission, spelt the end for the Commission: 'It is becoming difficult to find anyone who has even the slightest sense of responsibility'.

The Dutch commissioner, Mr Van den Broek, feels aggrieved. He described the comment as unfair and unjustified. 'It is not backed up by any of the findings elsewhere in the report. I have not kept count of the times I have been at the Parliament or before parliamentary committees, but what was that if it was not taking responsibility?'

ALGEMEEN DAGBLAD, *17 MARCH 1999*

The Belgian press was full of the Belgian Commissioner, Karel Van Miert, arguing that it was not fair that he should be blamed for other people's misconduct when he had always done his job properly:

'It is being made to look as though everything went wrong. There is no mention of departments where things are run properly. That is not fair'... It is true that Van Miert is a good commissioner, at least when it comes to his own empire. But that is not what the report is about. He is doing exactly what the five independent experts are criticising the Commission for: the commissioners each protect their own little territories and take no interest in what their colleagues are up to. As a member of the Commission Van Miert should also have paid attention to the work of the Commission as a whole. After all he was there too when another new project or ambitious programme was set up without the resources to implement it properly or to control expenditure

DE TELEGRAAF, 17 MARCH 1999

'They are talking like lawyers, not independent experts', he said ...Karel van Miert feels he has been badly treated ... It is 1 o'clock on Tuesday morning, a quarter of an hour after Commission President Jacques Santer read out the brief statement announcing the Commission's resignation. He looks pale ... Van Miert says, 'We had agreed to go along with the report's conclusions. We thought it would mainly criticise individual commissioners. Apart from one instance the result is much better than you might have expected after what people have been saying and writing over the past few months. Look at how Manuel Marin comes out of it. People have been writing all sorts of things about him. You have to feel for him. The Wise Men say that there was no fraud or personal financial gain involved. Only in one case did someone obviously go too far ... But even then they came to generalised conclusions that no one had anticipated, including President Santer. As far as I am concerned the conclusions are unacceptable. The committee says nothing about the parts of the Commission that work well, such as my departments ... the Commission has been making strenuous efforts to achieve that ...' It was only when he talked about the part of the report in which he was personally criticised that Van Miert became really angry. The experts allege that as the commissioner responsible for personnel matters he failed to take disciplinary action against two officials in the tourism case. 'Just imagine, that was put in without me having any contact at all with the experts. No phone call, no conversation, no hint, nothing. But the people who know what it's like know better. They know very well that I wanted to

intervene, but the problem in this place is the trade unions. They're the ones in control. So I would say that this is not a balanced report ... They have drawn general conclusions without looking at each department individually'.

HET NIEUWSBLAD, 17 MARCH 1999

What did Hans van den Broek, the Dutch Commissioner, think about what had happened? He was more non-committal:

According to Van den Broek, the Wise Men's report and particularly that one sentence on the very last page before the annexes came 'like a bolt from the blue ... On the Monday morning we were saying to each other that it was hard but we would come through it. No one, not even President Santer, had seen the general conclusions'. The commissioners all count themselves lucky that it was stated in black and white that there was no question of personal gain, even for those whose work was criticised. 'My departments come out of it well', says Van den Broek, who was earlier under attack by the Court of Auditors over his Central and Eastern European aid programmes.

'That is a source of satisfaction to me, although it does not make the end of this Commission any less sad. On Sunday he objected to a passage in the report referring to him. It was amended without protest.

ALGEMEEN DAGBLAD, 17 MARCH 1999

Even Trojan came in for criticism:

The Dutch Christian Democratic Alliance is also calling for the resignation of Carlo Trojan, who as Secretary-General was in charge of the Commission's administration.

The delegation claims that Trojan refused to listen to van Buitenen's complaints and tried to make van Buitenen look small by referring to him as 'just a junior official'. Commissioner Cresson even spread the rumour that van Buitenen was suffering from psychological problems because he had failed to get promoted.

Trojan is now saying that he was not responsible for van Buitenen's suspension; according to him the decision was taken by the Director-General of personnel and the Financial Controller director and he is therefore refusing to resign. Yesterday morning Hanja Maij-Weggen, leader of the CDA delegation, called for Trojan's resignation. Trojan is furious, alleging that Maij-Weggen is only out to 'deprive a Dutchman of a senior European post'. Commissioner Van den Broek backs him up. 'The administration is not immune, but there are procedures for taking action. Just because there is a crisis it does not mean we should start hitting out at everybody in sight'

ALGEMEEN DAGBLAD, 17 MARCH 1999

Back in the Picture

When I was asked to appear on a television programme with some of the commissioners I was wary and reluctant to get into a debate with members of the outgoing Commission. I had to be careful not to make any political statements, although I couldn't help saying that I disagreed with the aggrieved comments made for instance by Karel van Miert and Hans Van den Broek. After all the Commission was purposely organised so that all the commissioners were collectively responsible for decisions, specifically to protect them against national influence. In that they had failed to take any action they were all equally guilty. It is not enough simply to write a letter to a colleague about misconduct.

It was unwise of me to say that, but sometimes it just got too much for me. I was in an extremely vulnerable position; I had still had no indication what was going to happen to me in the Commission, even though I had repeatedly asked to go back to my normal work or at least be given an appropriate job in the Commission. I was afraid of being 'kicked upstairs' to a job with a nice office, a pen and a good view where I couldn't do anything. I just wanted to go back to where I was before. There was still so much to investigate ...

In the meantime there were calls for my rehabilitation:

The CDA delegation in the European Parliament says that Paul van Buitenen, the suspended European Commission official, ... must be given back his job and the pay that has been withheld. The Flemish Greens are also call-ing for his full rehabilitation … Van Buitenen wants 'whistleblowers' such as himself to be better protected in future. His own position remains uncertain. 'I am still hanging on by the skin of my teeth'.

ALGEMEEN DAGBLAD, 17 MARCH 1999

Not only should van Buitenen go straight back to work, he deserves full reha-bilitation and an apology for what has been done to him.

DE MORGEN, YVES DESMET, 17 MARCH 1999

Edith: 'That was typical of what was going on at the time. We thought the misery of uncertainty about the future would be over. Everyone was congratulating Paul. We were given flowers, cards and even bottles of champagne by col-leagues who had bet that Paul would never manage to get any of the commissioners removed, let alone the whole Commission! But in practice the Commission unfortu-nately hung on to all its powers and obviously there was no one in that Commission who felt inclined to hail Paul as a hero. Our euphoria was short-lived. When there was no news from Brussels, we suspected the worst; it was quite likely that nothing would change as far as Paul was con-cerned'.

Mixed Reaction

On 18 March I was due to go to a big meeting of all the staff unions in the Commission. My union had phoned me because my fellow union members were going to draw up a resolution at the meeting calling for my immediate return to work.

At the time I was not at all well. I felt sick and my head and stomach ached. As I walked along the corridors to the hall I saw the surreptitious glances. Some people were courageous enough to greet me openly; others acted as if they hadn't seen me.

The meeting hall was packed with more than a thousand Commission staff. In fact some people had to follow the meeting outside on the monitors. I walked towards the front through the crowds of officials with my lawyer. Suddenly the chairman of my union saw me coming. He immediately interrupted the speeches and announced me. Thunderous applause broke out.

'Thank goodness', I thought to myself. 'They're on my side, I haven't wasted my time coming'.

As I walked forward as if in a daze I could hear the cameramen jostling for position.

The applause continued, but all over the hall I could also see people who were making a point of not clapping. That was confusing. Everyone there was either for me or against me.

I walked up Franco Ianniello, who had earlier announced me. I had to thank him. Franco and I hugged and kissed each other. It was the first time I had ever greeted another man like that, but it gave me a good feeling. It was nice to know I had 'comrades in arms'.

A little while later, when the meeting came to 'any other business', I was asked to say a few words. I kept it simple and just said that I wanted my old job in Financial Control back. This was greeted with applause and approval and put into a resolution.

But still I was not rehabilitated. It was a bitter disappointment. My mood changed. I was worn out and in interviews I became weary, dejected and angry:

He does not look well. It is obvious from the circles under his eyes that the past few months have taken their toll on the suspended European official Paul van Buitenen. 'I have a headache and I feel edgy', he says when anyone remarks on his appearance.

'The last few months have been almost indescribable. Of course I had doubts at times, especially when commissioners like Cresson, Santer and Van

den Broek made comments about me in public. It was alleged that I was incompetent and that I was setting myself up as a policeman, judge and prosecutor at the same time. Sometimes the remarks were actually slanderous.

... I had expected a transfer or a setback to my career . But no, they tried to discredit me. Luckily it didn't work, though. Do you know what I would like? A statement from Santer that he was wrong and that I can come back. I did write to him. Was I expecting a reply? I don't think so. I have now heard on the grapevine that I can come back when the new Commission president is named.' So the uncertainty about his future continues. Van Buitenen says, 'On 16 April the suspension period ends. I am on half-pay at the moment but in any case they have to pay my full salary again after that. The suspension can continue. I'll wait and see'. He also wants his duty of confidentiality waived. 'There are indications—although I have no proof, mind you—that the legal authorities have not been given the information they need for the cases they are still investigating. The authorities want to speak to me about it but I am not allowed to talk to them because I am bound by professional secrecy'. So are there more revelations about misconduct still to come?

'I'm not saying that', he replies sharply. 'I don't want to play the hero and try and force the issue. If I am allowed to work, it will happen anyway. That's why I want the same job and everything that goes with it. Full powers as an auditor and access to all the information systems I need'.

BRABANTS NIEUWSBLAD/DE STEM, 18 MARCH 1999

On 23 March Parliament was to debate and vote on the Wise Men's report and the Commission's resignation. The day before that I wrote to a number of MEPs in the hope of gaining support from Parliament for my rehabilitation. The following are extracts from the letter:

To Members of the European Parliament and chairmen of the Committee on Budgetary Control,

I am writing this letter to draw your attention to my personal situation and seek your support for my reinstatement. I am still under suspension on half-pay ... In December I sent my letter to

Parliament through the Greens. I had good reasons for doing this. They did pass the letter on immediately to the other political groups but I can appreciate that other groups were upset that they did not have access to the letter with the annexes from the start. Now I would do things differently ...

I am a genuine whistleblower. I acted in good faith, I was not seeking any personal advantage and I initially informed my superiors fully in strict accordance with the rules. This was in line with the official criteria for the protection of whistleblowers that operate in the United Kingdom. Furthermore my letter was backed up by the Committee of Independent Experts' report ... I have been severely penalised, as if I had committed a serious offence ... Commissioners have slandered me without my being able to defend myself. I have reason to believe that the Commission is not cooperating fully with the Belgian judicial authorities and is in fact hampering the investigations. My request for my professional secrecy to be waived has been refused, so that I cannot be interviewed by the Belgian judicial authorities ... I ask all the political groups in Parliament to support my rehabilitation and reinstatement in Financial Control. The disciplinary proceedings against me should be ended. If there are still problems in the Commission I would be glad to come and work as an official in Parliament at the same grade as I had in the Commission. I sincerely hope that a solution can be found, regardless of political differences, since I assume you are all in favour of protection for genuine whistleblowers. I thank you for any clear signs you are able to give me.

The Mood Cools

By the time the contents of the report were debated, the tension had been considerably defused by the Commission's resignation.

The debate had been planned in advance so that any further vote of no confidence could be discussed and voted on. However the Commission salvaged its reputation at the last moment as soon as it realised that there was no longer a parliamentary majority in favour of its remaining in office. That made it look as though the MEPs were talking about an issue that had already been decided. Obviously that was not the case though, because there were still important matters to be discussed. Would the Wise Men be allowed to carry on? Would they be able to investigate the Parliament as well? How would a new Commission be appointed? And what was to happen about van Buitenen? These were all questions that needed to be answered.

In the meantime the Wise Men had still only produced a limited first interim report on the personal responsibility of individual commissioners. There was still a great deal to be looked into before they could come up with recommendations to prevent similar problems in the future, for instance the political appointments at the top of the administration and the position of whistleblowers. Parliament set a deadline of early September for the second report on the practices in the Commission. This second report was only to focus on the recommendations to be made. Individual cases of irregularities could not be addressed anymore. It also decided that the Committee should not look into possible misconduct in Parliament. To my mind that was a missed opportunity.

My position also came up in the parliamentary debates and votes. A particular passage referring to my position was discussed at great length before the vote on the outcome of the Wise Men's report and the Commission's resignation. The first proposal by the Greens was clearly worded. This version went further than the others but in my view it was still moderate. It asked the President of the European Parliament to take the necessary

steps with the Commission and Council for me to be fully reinstated in a suitable post in the European institutions, paid the
salary that had been withheld and have my immunity waived as
the Belgian legal authorities were asking so that I could be interviewed as a witness in the cases still under investigation.

It was soon clear from the discussions with the large political
groups (the Socialists and Christian Democrats) that this went
much too far for them and it was rejected. Nelly Maes and her
assistant Bart Staes from the Belgian Volksunie had in the meantime prepared an alternative version for this eventuality which
was less specific. This version also had the backing of the Greens
and a number of MEPs from the Dutch and Belgian Socialist and
Liberal parties in particular and the small Christian parties. Jens-
Peter Bonde from the Danish June Movement also played an
important part. The toned down version asked the Commission
to review my position in the light of recent developments and
decide on the best possible outcome for me.

This version was not adopted either. Finally Magda Aelvoet
(on behalf of the Greens) and Jens-Peter Bonde (on behalf of the
Europe of the Nations Group) tabled a very slight amendment.
The Commission was asked to review my case following the
report and its conclusions.

In the end Parliament adopted this very superficial and non-
committal wording. Another proposal was then put forward for
a separate article to be incorporated in the Staff Regulations to
protect whistleblowers. This was rejected with over 400 votes
against and about 90 in favour. I felt completely let down. The
attitude of the two biggest political groups, the Socialists and the
Christian Democrats, was particularly disappointing and I made
that clear to the press:

> In van Buitenen's view this was 'shameful'. The Greens had put forward pro-
> posals to help him get a suitable job. They were rejected because the two largest

Edith: 'I could see that Paul was at the end of his tether. I was very worried about him. He was at home under sus-pension but he had never been so busy in his life. He was working on reports, giving interviews in four languages and he had to look carefully at every word with his legal advisers because anything could be used against him. This had already been going on for months and it was a mys-tery to me how he kept it up. Most nights he only had about four or five hours sleep. At one point when he was giving his umpteenth telephone interview I could see that he was absolutely dead beat. He was looking very pale and rubbing his forehead. I whispered to him in the middle of the interview, "Why don't you just unplug the phone for a little while after this and get a bit of rest?" He nodded wearily and gratefully, as if he could only rest when some-one else told him to.

I was very concerned about his health. It really seemed as if once the Wise Men's report was published it was the end of the road for Paul emotionally, as if he felt that he could now collapse.

In the next few weeks there was complete silence from the Commission. It was just as though Paul didn't exist. That lasted exactly a month. After that the four month period was up. That was the maximum time he could be suspended with his salary withheld and then they had to do something'.

CHAPTER TEN

A New Job

When Joep Dohmen's book *Europese Idealisten* was published I understood why the largest political groups in the European Parliament were less than enthusiastic about supporting a whistleblower. The book exposed cases of favouritism and corruption by MEPs. These included claiming attendance allowances for sittings they had not attended (SiSo or Sign in Sod off), the unauthorised use of private chauffeurs and official cars, conflicts of interest between their membership of parliamentary committees and their association with certain firms, family members based abroad being paid as assistants and the role of masonic lodges. To my mind the most shocking example was the political appointment of a director-general nominated by one of the large political groups. The other large political group was prepared to go along with that if it could put forward its own director-general, but there was only one vacant post. No problem. A DG was divided, instantly creating two vacant posts. I often thought of that later when my own case was under consideration. Apparently that was a bit more difficult to resolve.

I took Dohmen's book on holiday with me. Now that things had calmed down a little Edith and I thought we could make up for our disastrous Christmas holiday and take a couple of days off.

Edith: 'We went to Thermae-2000 in the Dutch province of Limburg. As it happened they had recently had a problem with legionnaire's disease. A lot of people had cancelled and it was unusually quiet. We thought that after that it must be the most thoroughly inspected spa in the country and we enjoyed the unexpected luxury and peace. On the third day of our stay my mother rang us up in great excitement. "Someone from the Commission rang wanting to speak to Paul. It's about his future and it sounded really promising!" We almost cut our brief holiday short to go and find out what was happening. Luckily Paul decided that after our family had gone through four months of stress the Commission could easily wait another two days'.

Transferred

I did not feel all that rested after my short holiday. Even though I had been under suspension, with the press, the debates and all the stress surrounding them I had never been so busy as in the last few months. Nevertheless I was keen to get back to work as usual. So that day, in good spirits and eager to know what was happening, I contacted the director-general of personnel who had rung and asked to speak to me. In any case the period for which they were allowed to keep me on half pay was over.

The director-general did not have good news for me. I could certainly go back to work but not to my old post in Financial Control. I was being given a management job in the buildings department. I would not be allowed to work in my old unit in Financial Control. I was also told specifically that this did not mean I was being let off the hook; the disciplinary proceedings would continue. I was to return to work straightaway the following Monday but that same afternoon I would be interviewed again for the disciplinary proceedings.

The Commission could have stopped the disciplinary proceedings after the preliminary official investigation was over. I knew that had often happened before, in some cases when the official concerned had been guilty of serious irregularities, and this I found very hard to take. Even if the Commission still insisted that I was in the wrong it would have been possible to plead extenuating circumstances. There was every justification for doing so in my case. I tried to defuse the situation by suggesting that I could accept a light punishment (censure or a reprimand) and even leave the Commission after that if necessary to be transferred to another EU institution. However the Commission had decided to carry on with the internal disciplinary proceedings. So the threat of dismissal had still not been lifted.

The feeling of disappointment and powerlessness was made worse by the fact that journalists were ringing all the time to congratulate me on how well things had turned out. I had no idea what they were talking about. I thought they clearly hadn't a clue what was going on. It was not until a couple of days later that I heard that the Commission had issued a press release saying I had been promoted and was back at work. There was no mention of the disciplinary proceedings, which could have simply been brought to an end after the independent experts' report. I only realised when I saw the Dutch Lower House debating my case on TV that the disciplinary proceedings against me were still not being stopped.

So it was left to me to correct the misconceptions in the press and the European Parliament and explain that things were by no means settled. I was not going to be hushed up!

'I was still secretly hoping that the Commission would have come to its senses in the meantime and that I could go back to my old job, temporarily if need be', van Buitenen told De Morgen yesterday. 'Under the regulations a decision *has to be taken after four months' suspension. Obviously they decided on a position that would pose the least possible risk to them. Officially I am being transferred because working relationships in the financial control branch would be disrupted. That's rubbish. My boss and my colleagues are quite happy to go on working with me'. In the meantime the disciplinary proceedings against van Buitenen are continuing, so he is still threatened with punishment, which might be anything from a reprimand to dismissal. Volksunie MEP Nelly Maes finds it extraordinary that the Commission is treating the transfer as part of an 'ongoing case'.*

DE MORGEN, 14 APRIL 1999

Back to Work Again

All the same it was wonderful to get back to the regular routine of a working week. I drove to Brussels bright and early on the Monday morning. I was given a friendly welcome in the buildings department and a lot of people came and shook me by the hand. I was determined to start my new job as a loyal employee, even if I was not all that happy about it.

After a couple of days later I really started to miss the real work in financial control. I had no access now to particular computer systems and there were still so many things to be investigated. I had the files at home and I was still getting loads of information from all over Europe. Was I going to have to give all that up?

The new job was not easy. I had never done this kind of work before and there was a very strict deadline. I had five months to set up a new unit and have a new computer system developed and ready for use. Ultimately I would also have to lead a team that had not yet been created. I was faced with a task that would have been difficult even under normal circumstances. With my priorities elsewhere and disciplinary proceedings hanging over me the situation was absolutely impossible. My colleagues in the buildings department were well-meaning and very pleasant but I felt out of place. I saw it as a way of keeping me quiet.

It was a strange period. Only a few weeks before I had been awarded a prize in Copenhagen for standing up for my convictions and had been hailed as a hero. Now I was in a backwater in the Commission with a job that I didn't belong in.

At the end of April I wrote a letter to my new director saying that I was unhappy with this new situation. I sent copies of the letter to various other people in the hierarchy, including my director-general, Mr Jansen.

I said I should have been sent back to my old job and I regarded the Commission's action as unnecessarily punitive. It seemed to be an attempt to stop me coming out with further revelations. I explained that for that reason I would prefer not to stay in the new job and in any case I did not have the experience and qualifications to do the job properly. I promised I would do my best, but I strongly advised my superiors to find someone better qualified for the job.

I also pointed out how complicated my position was because of the ongoing disciplinary proceedings, which were taking up a great deal of my time and attention. I was still being interviewed, both for the disciplinary proceedings and by the Committee of Wise Men.

This letter was the start of a long and acrimonious correspondence between me and my director-general.

Interview

My work in the buildings department was interspersed with interviews for the disciplinary proceedings. For these I had to go to Mr Berger's office in another Commission building. I had a lawyer with me.

The interviews were very formal and were aimed at getting as much information as possible. I was pleased at the care that was taken; it put me on my mettle to have the facts looked at again in detail. At my request the interviews were conducted in Dutch.

For instance I was questioned about how I had got documents from DG XXII when I was actually working in Financial Control. I said I sometimes got documents from former colleagues, sometimes they turned up in my office and some came to me from outside the Commission. Other people sent me documents, in some cases anonymously. I could appreciate that they wanted names, but obviously I could not give them any. It was an unpleasant situation. Unless I could prove that people had given the documents to me voluntarily I could be accused of stealing them. Not really knowing what to do, I remained non-committal. I said I would check the source of all the documents but without giving any names.

Step by step the investigators went back over everything I had done in the past year, but I could honestly say to them that I had done all I could to report the problems through the normal channels, through my head of department, my director-general, UCLAF and finally the secretary-general, before going to the European Parliament. I also explained how upset I was when Parliament considered the Leonardo II proposals without being given any hint of what had gone wrong in the previous programme. The investigators thought the problems with the Leonardo programme were mainly related to the TAO but I said that the issue was much wider and had its roots in DG XXII's management.

They were also interested in why I had raised other matters as well as Leonardo in the letter I sent in December. I was trying to show that this was an institutional problem. The Commission always waited too long before starting audits or investigations. Apart from that the investigations achieved very little although in all these cases there were reliable indications of mismanagement in the DGs or programmes. Where there were good audit reports available, the proper follow-up by the hierarchy was lacking. I had deliberately chosen examples that had been going on for some time. My aim was to show that the Commission was not doing enough to resolve the problems and the information it gave Parliament, the Court of Auditors and the judicial authorities was too little, too late.

Queen's Birthday

Since my letter to the European Parliament was published, the Brussels 'in crowd' had had a curiously ambivalent attitude to me. Everyone was either for me or against me. Sometimes colleagues ignored me or avoided me in company but then later, in private, expressed their sympathy. When that happened I didn't know how to react. I was particularly perplexed when I went into Mr Ridley's office one day. He was a colleague I had always got on well with. He dashed out, ran into his department and brought another colleague into his room. Only then did he sit down and say, 'What can I do for you, Paul?'

This year Edith and I went to the Queen's Birthday reception in the Orangerie for the second time. This annual event was organised by the permanent representation of the Netherlands and attended by many Dutch people in the Commission. Someone from one of the audit departments came up to me and expressed his admiration for what I had done. 'There is still a lot that has not come out. I must speak to you, but I have to sort out something with my hierarchy first. I wish you luck, Mr van Buitenen'. I was immediately curious.

Our names were announced to the ambassador. I could see he was looking at me while he was still talking to someone else and that he recognised me. What was he thinking? Did I fit in at his little gathering? Then it was our turn. He greeted us and let me know in official terms that he was aware of who I was.

We moved on and mingled with the crowd. Fortunately no one avoided us. Various people spoke to us, including the vice chairman of a large company who said he would like to speak to me but he wanted to come to an arrangement about what I would do with the information. 'Well', I thought to myself, 'things must go wrong in big organisations like that sometimes as well'. A lot of people we didn't know spoke to us, as well as colleagues and politicians. It was a strange experience. There I was surrounded by Dutch people who had some kind of role in the Commission. While we were having an informal drink they were cordial, but soon they would all be taking up their positions again. What did they still have up their sleeves for me?

Official Silence

At the beginning of May I got a reply to my letter from my director-general, Mr Jansen, saying that the transfer to a post commensurate with my grade and classification was perfectly legal and had been taken in the interests of the Commission service. What he was really saying was that I should stop moaning and get on with my work!

Fair enough, I could appreciate his point of view. But as I read on my amazement grew. Jansen, citing the Staff Regulations, told me I should go through official channels with my information on fraud and irregularities. He said that in the light of my obligations under the Staff Regulations he was asking me to hand over any information I had about possible fraud, irregularities and mismanagement. He was also expecting me to notify him of any information I intended to pass on to the European Parliament's Committee, the European Court of Auditors or any other body or to the press. Whether approval could be granted under those provisions depended on the information to be passed on.

What I was going to do now? Allow myself to be hushed up? In any case I had already revealed the most important cases and was assisting with the Wise Men's investigation. Obviously he wanted to have total control over whatever action I decided to take.

The Committee

I had initially requested a further interview with the Committee of Wise Men at the end of May. First of all I wanted to finish my contributions on various matters that needed further investigation so that the questions could focus more directly on the new material. However the secretary rang to ask if I could come earlier. The experts would very much like to see me in the near future. I wondered why and hoped it was about a transfer to the Committee's secretariat. That would be almost too good to be true. I often cherished these hopes over the months. I longed to be in a job where I could settle down and make a really useful contribution.

The visit to the Committee was much more informal and less worrying than the first time. I went on my own, without a lawyer. Two experts and an English-speaking colleague greeted me.

Although it was never said in so many words, I gathered from the conversation that very few other Commission officials had availed themselves of the opportunity to give information to the Committee of Wise Men. The Wise Men's formal assurances of confidentiality had obviously not been a sufficient incentive. So hadn't they called the people whose names I had given them last time? Yes, they had been called but they had not provided any specific information.

Obviously the Committee was not getting enough cooperation from people in the Commission. Was that why they had
asked me back again so soon?

It was like a slap in the face for me. I was terribly disillusioned. No one was prepared to stick their necks out; they just
left it all to me.

The expert who was looking into the Leonardo case asked
me to write a report on my findings. I agreed, although afterwards I realised it would take up a lot of my spare time.

That afternoon, with my consent, we had a visit at home from
the Brussels Criminal Investigation Police's anti-corruption unit.
It appeared from the interview that the Commission was not
cooperating fully with the Belgian judicial authorities and the
investigation was in danger of grinding to a halt before it had
begun. I realised that I still had a lot of work to do.

Edith: Paul could not stop helping in the investigations
because if he did they would peter out and it would all
have been for nothing. He began getting pains in his head
and stomach whenever he had to go to work. He found
his work in the buildings department a waste of time. With
his lawyer's help he wrote a letter of protest against his
unwanted transfer, saying that it was making him physically ill. He also asked to be given back his old job in
Financial Control. After all the independent experts' report
had shown that his claims were—to put it mildly—justified. The Commission owed him a full explanation as to
why he was now being penalised with a transfer and why
the disciplinary proceedings were continuing.

Sick Leave

Once again I received an official reply to the letter, saying that my transfer was in the interests of the Commission Service and if I was physically ill I should go to the doctor.

I followed that advice. I felt really terrible and started having physical symptoms. Our GP was not surprised; he had been expecting me. 'Every time my surgery door opens I think it's going to be you, complaining of insomnia at the very least. I am amazed you have managed to keep going'.

We had a long talk, at the end of which the doctor told me to take four weeks off. He was concerned about what would happen after that. He kept saying that there must be some prospect of a reasonable solution. Obviously four weeks at home took the immediate pressure off and averted the risk of collapse but it was not a permanent solution.

For the time being things were good. Straightaway I was relieved of a burden. I made another appointment with one of the Commission doctors, who agreed with the GP. He was worried that I had too much on my plate. His advice was, 'Do a little bit of work on the reports you say have to be written but take plenty of rest. Set yourself a deadline for the reports and stick to it. Otherwise there will be no point in taking time off'. He too was very concerned and wanted me to come back regularly so that he could monitor my progress.

Edith: 'Paul perked up immediately. He worked for part of the day and after that he tried to relax, which was not easy after all those months of non-stop emotional stress. He was still getting constant phone calls from interested journalists'.

Two weeks later I got a registered letter from the Commission, one of many I received in that period. I was to make an appointment with a Commission doctor straightaway.

That was not normal; officials could often be away on sick leave for ages without anyone checking up on them. But I had to report more or less immediately. I went and explained what was wrong with me, but the doctor said I could easily work with a headache and stomach ache. 'Can't you come up with anything more serious than that?' I was not prepared to think up a fictitious illness. 'If you think that I am not under unusual pressure at the moment and that I can work even though I'm ill, you'll have to put that in your report'. In the corridor I met the other doctor I had seen earlier, who was very surprised at what was happening.

> *Edith*: 'Paul had hardly ever been ill before. Two doctors had said he should take it easy but this third doctor, without any consultation with the first two, decided otherwise. The Commission accepted the last diagnosis thankfully. A registered letter from the Commission quickly followed. Actually on his birthday, Paul was told he had to go back to work straightaway. What was more all the sick leave he had had was to be deducted from his annual leave! And if he did not have enough leave left it would have to be deducted from his salary. We were aghast. This was the Commission everyone in Europe thought had resigned but behind the scenes it was still playing the same old cat and mouse game with Paul. Paul's lawyer started writing his umpteenth letter of protest. Another thing we noticed was that it took the Commission weeks or months to reply to Paul's letters of protest whereas anything that could be used against him was dealt with in a flash'.

Pointless Tug of War

In reply to the director-general's letter I sent a fairly disgruntled letter of protest, saying that I was loyal to the Commission but that his letter forbade me to do anything and gave me absolutely no scope for action in my difficult situation. I was having to write a report for the Committee of Wise Men, help the legal authorities, work on my own defence and also keep in contact with other bodies and the press. At the same time I was trying to be as fair as possible to the organisation. And finally, I said, I was physically and mentally collapsing under the strain.

They refused to accept that I was ill. A few weeks later Jansen sent me a letter saying that he understood from recent articles in the press that I had said I was writing a second report for the Committee of Wise Men containing evidence of fraud, corruption and other serious irregularities. He reminded me of my obligations under Article 7 of the Commission's decision of 18 July 1998, to which he had drawn my attention in his letter of 30 April 1999. If I had any such evidence I was to notify him as my director-general, or alternatively UCLAF. He also reminded me that I had to obtain his permission before taking part in any interviews or meetings; if not I would be contravening the Staff Regulations.

So the wrangling between me and Jansen continued: about my sick leave and annual leave, my contacts with the press, the fact that I reported to the Wise Men (and therefore not to him), and so on and so on. I also wrote to the medical department protesting at the conflicting opinions given by the doctors.

In the middle of June I received a copy of a letter from one of Jansen's senior officials. He had tipped my director-general off that I was reported to have been in my old office in Financial Control in office hours. I had to read the letter (which was in French) three times before I could believe it. So my movements were being watched and reported to my director-general. I had only been to see my ex-colleagues because I was going for a meal with them. I was furious and wrote an angry letter to Jansen saying that in my opinion that was no way to treat people.

I wrote another letter to Jansen in which I said that I was going to take very good care that the information ended up in the right place and in my view that was not, in the first instance, with him:

I am working with the Committee of Wise Men, the Belgian legal authorities and where necessary with OLAF. I do not think that at this stage it is necessary to coordinate my work with you, given that you have no authority in this area and I am an anxious to avoid any more unnecessary hindrance to the current investigations. The only way you can normalise the situation is to put me back in Internal Audit in Financial Control, or better still in OLAF, in the interests of the Commission service.

Eventually I got a fairly mild note from Jansen in which he actually left the decision on my attendance at work to my head of department. That was the end of the matter for the time being. But this whole rigmarole had cost me more blood, sweat and tears.

At the end of June I did lodge a formal appeal against my transfer, although I had no confidence at all in the internal procedures. I did this as a safeguard before the three-month appeal period was up so that I didn't forfeit my formal rights.

Bringing in the Media

So I was not supposed to speak to the media? I didn't even have to think about that. It was quite clear to me now that the only place I was going to get any support was from the media. I told anyone who was prepared to listen what had happened to me in the Brussels hornets' nest:

'As a matter of principle I want to go back to my job in Financial Control, even if it's only for a short time', says van Buitenen. 'The Commission has to admit publicly that I have not done anything wrong'.

But whether that will happen is the big question. 'I can't stand up to the Commission on my own. If they keep it up for long enough they can ruin my career', he says. Van Buitenen returned to work at the Commission in the middle of April after his suspension. Not to his old job in Financial Control but to the buildings department, where things are not going well for him. The events of the past few months and the disciplinary proceedings that are still continuing are taking their toll, so much so that his health is suffering. His GP advised him to rest. The Commission's medical service agreed. But at the end of last week the Commission sent him to a third doctor, who declared him fit and sent him back to work. He then received a letter saying that his absence was unauthorised and all the sick leave would be deducted from his salary. 'I feel like a small cog in a big machine that is trying to crush me'. The European Commission, perhaps afraid of more dirty linen being revealed, is trying to silence its official. Van Buitenen himself hints that there are more fireworks to come. 'The Commission has stepped down. Everyone thinks the problem is solved now and I will be satisfied. But that's simply not true', he says. At the moment he is working hard on two reports, one on his own initiative and another for the Committee of Wise Men. 'I want to draw attention to various issues that have not been properly clarified', says van Buitenen. 'They raise the question of whether disciplinary proceedings should be taken against a number of senior officials'. He always prints out his reports and makes backup copies, which are left with friends or in a safe. 'I don't want to run the risk of someone later being put under pressure and funny things happening or my stuff being stolen', he says. After the first report the Commission led by President Jacques Santer was forced to resign. The Wise Men's second report, due in September, examines what is wrong in the Commission in more detail. The Committee will suggest institutional improvements. Van Buitenen believes that the Committee is being hampered in its investigation. 'I suspect that quite a lot of officials are not telling what they know'. He does not think the committee has enough powers. 'It should be able to interview people under oath. Then officials would have to lie under oath. Most officials don't do that'.

Worse still is the fact that the Commission is not cooperating fully with the police investigation into the Leonardo da Vinci irregularities. The case was taken up by Nelly Maes (VU). 'The police carried out a search here, with my *consent, to get the information they need'. Van Buitenen wants everything fully investigated. 'People are making fine speeches at the moment about the fight against fraud and greater openness, including Prodi (the new Commission President). But I want to see something done'. Van Buitenen cannot keep up his opposition for much longer. 'I hope I can count on support from the European Parliament. If not, I'm finished'.*

Photo caption: 'I have a strong sense of justice. My Christian faith gives me the strength to go on. It makes me feel that I am not alone'

DE MORGEN, 5 JUNE 1999

Ongoing Investigation

All the Commission letters were sent to my home address by registered post. Usually they were formal letters from Jansen reminding me of my duties and imposing restrictions on me. But one day I got a very welcome communication: the decision to waive my professional secrecy on the tourism case so that I could make a witness statement to the Belgian legal authorities.

At last. I was wondering what had happened to the decision. My immunity was only lifted for that particular case. I was still not allowed to hand over evidence on any other cases voluntarily to the Belgian authorities. There was still a danger that the evidence would be ruled invalid.

Within a month I was able to let the Committee of Wise Men have a draft of my report. I had made it a personal report, asking the Committee in the introduction to spare a thought for my predicament. The report was not yet complete and there were still a few annexes missing, but in the meantime here was something they could get to work on. I referred to a hundred background documents in all. I warned the Committee to be careful with the information and treat it as confidential because a number of sources were named. I asked them not to pass the report on to the European Commission for fear that it might make improper use of it in my disciplinary proceedings. I was also afraid it might be used as a basis for disciplinary proceedings against other officials.

CHAPTER ELEVEN

Dentist Under Investigation

At the end of 1998 there was a stir in the press about a case of alleged favouritism. The journalists had hard facts and I wondered afterwards how they had got hold of them. Rumours had already been circulating in the Commission for some time. René Berthelot, a French dentist, had been awarded contracts with the Commission for work for which he was totally unqualified. He could not actually do the work, nor indeed did he do it. It was apparently Commissioner Cresson who had secured the contracts for Berthelot, despite his lack of credentials.

People gossiped about Berthelot and Cresson in the Commission. Everyone knew that they lived at the same address in Brussels. There was a rumour that at a meeting with Commission officials in Cresson's office Berthelot had sat at the commissioner's desk smoking a cigar with his feet up on the desk and told the visitors that that was really his seat.

A lot of people in the Commission departments concerned already knew something of what was going on or had heard of Berthelot being involved in various irregularities, but everyone kept quiet. There was talk in the corridors but since the matter was so sensitive and directly affected a Commissioner's position it was extremely dangerous to try and do anything about it. Eventually someone must have leaked the story to the press and smuggled out incriminating material.

When I was writing the letter that I eventually sent to the European Parliament in November 1998 I knew comparatively little about this case and had not heard most of the rumours. Although I mentioned Berthelot several times in my letter I had nothing to back up the stories. One sentence in my report indicated how far the scandal actually went, although I did not realise it myself at the time. I said that a colleague had told me that another serious irregularity connected with Cresson had been discovered during an internal audit. My colleagues were unwilling to say any more because they were afraid I would report it. Apparently they had been ordered to keep quiet about it.

Stories in the Press

The allegations in the press continued and they were quite serious. It was widely reported that in 1997 Berthelot had been appointed as a scientific adviser to do a year's research into AIDS for one of Mrs Cresson's programmes at a fee of about £4,000 a month. Berthelot was a dentist who, judging from lists of international medical publications, had never had anything to do with AIDS research before. 'There must at least have been a procedural irregularity'.

Further reports appeared in the press. The contract with Berthelot started in March 1997. Unfortunately he was unable to do any research because in April he had a heart attack. He was unfit for work and had to have a quadruple bypass operation. In the meantime the contract just continued and he still got paid. Berthelot did not cancel the contract so the research simply came to a halt. No one said anything. It was not until eight months later, in December 1997, that Berthelot requested the termination of his contract.

In 1998 an internal audit by DG XX soon discovered what

was going on, but what was done about this information in the Commission was not clear. Two senior officials advised that the money should be reclaimed, but Cresson apparently put a stop to that. She said she was 'satisfied with Berthelot's work'. Somehow or other the whole thing died down and no further action was taken.

Documents

I was not really surprised at what had happened. The name Berthelot had already cropped up quite a few times in connection with irregularities in my files on other matters. But I was surprised that the story came out. Belgian, German and Italian journalists seemed to have a wealth of information. They could produce copies of contracts and documents showing that Edith Cresson had dealt with the matter personally. The journalists were happy to let me have the material. They told me that UCLAF also had the documents.

According to the documents my former colleague Arnd Hanssen in DG XX had found out about the Berthelot contracts and the irregularities in the Joint Research Centre. Since Berthelot was unable to fulfil his contractual obligations our department had recommended that he be asked to return the money. Apparently our Director General, Mrs Speculanti, was reluctant to do anything. She took over and decided, in consultation with Mrs Cresson's cabinet, that the money should not be recovered. The file was put away. I gathered from colleagues in Financial Control that after Mrs Speculanti took charge they were expected to keep quiet about Berthelot.

Amongst the documents I found contracts between Berthelot and an offshore company called Kensington. The Commission used this arrangement to circumvent complicated social legislation when awarding contracts. I saw a contract between

Berthelot and Dony, the owner of the offshore company. There was also a sort of diary amongst the papers which showed that Dony had apparently let his Brussels flat to Berthelot through another company and was boasting to everyone that Berthelot lived there. As a result Berthelot left in a hurry in 1996 and moved in with Mrs Cresson. The papers also included some correspondence with lawyers which seemed to confirm the story about the flat.

It was quite a story. If the documents were true, things didn't look too good for Mrs Cresson, who at that point was still a commissioner.

Parliamentary Action

In February I spoke to a socialist MEP about the letter I had sent in December. He had contacted me to ask for information. He did not want it to look as though he supported Mrs Cresson just because they were both socialists. I thought that was commendable and I agreed to let him have the information he wanted. I told him about the documents the journalists had and he said he would like copies. I summarised the main points and handed them over. I had also drawn up a list of critical questions because I suspected there was more. The MEP agreed with my analysis and after looking at the file he contacted Mrs Speculanti about the handling of the Berthelot case. She had to explain why Berthelot had apparently not been asked to reimburse the money he had been paid and she showed him a file in which Berthelot reported to Cresson on his AIDS research work. These documents were sent to DG XX on 30 July 1998. According to Mrs Speculanti the reports clearly justified the payments to Berthelot throughout the period he had worked for Cresson's departments.

However the MEP was not satisfied with the explanation and

went on the attack. At the end of February he interrogated Mrs Cresson at the meeting of the budgetary control committee and he didn't stop there. At the meeting he distributed a set of copies of key documents about Berthelot, which were to be treated as confidential. He said some of the documents came from Mrs Speculanti. Mrs Speculanti hastily denied this at the meeting, but some of the people present could not be prevented from copying documents in the Parliament.

The press seized on the story:

Yesterday French EU Commissioner Edith Cresson came under heavy fire in two European Parliament control committees after further allegations of abuse of power. Cresson is alleged to have let a specialist on her private staff who evaluated tenders be awarded a lucrative contract. She also stopped Commission auditors recovering money from retired dentist René Berthelot, who lives with Cresson and was awarded a contract unlawfully.

Cresson responded indignantly to questions about Berthelot in the Committee on Budgetary Control. She originally recruited the French dentist through an offshore company. This arrangement enabled the Commission to pay certain staff and bypass the Belgian tax and social security authorities. Between February and August 1995 Berthelot was paid about £2,500 a month. In September 1995 he started working for the Commission direct as an expert on AIDS and biotechnology, even though he did not have the right qualifications. A. Osterhaus, a Rotterdam professor who checks the credentials of scientists for the Commission, alleged this on Monday evening in the Dutch television programme Netwerk.

Berthelot was paid around £3,500 a month, plus an extra 25% for his expertise. At the end of last year Cresson apparently took steps to prevent the recovery of a large part of those payments, even though the auditors backed the claim up with strong arguments.

Dutch EU official Paul van Buitenen, who was removed from his job at the end of last year after going public with files on Cresson's abuse of power, said he was aware of Mrs Cresson's action, revealed on Monday in the Dutch newspaper De Limburger.

Last week van Buitenen was interviewed by a Committee of Independent Experts which is to produce a report on the fraud cases next week.

In the morning Cresson had already made a poor impression in the European Parliament's Culture Committee. The committee's responsibilities include education and youth, areas in which, according to auditors' reports, the Socialist commissioner has also abused her position. Even members of the Socialist Group, who by their own account were still trying to save her from a lynching last month, have now turned against her.

'Although my questions were very specific and she was allowed to see them beforehand, her answers were very vague', says MEP Philippe de Coene (SP). 'We tried to give her an opportunity to defend herself but she missed her chance. I would not support her any more when it comes to the vote'.

One of the questions concerned her 1995 initiative to set up a 'cellule de communication', which was to contract work to outside firms for the provision of communications services. De Coene wanted more information about an expert who was allowed to draw up specifications for a call for tenders but later took part in the open tender procedure with her own company, Mayonic Public Relations, and won the contract. Between March 1997 and February 1998 the firm earned in the region of £175,000 from the Commission.

Yesterday Cresson flatly denied any conflict of interests 'because the expert had no decision-making powers in the call for tenders', but she failed to convince her audience. 'It was all done under the supervision of the head of her private office', says De Coene, 'and for that alone she should take political responsibility'.

DE MORGEN, 24 FEBRUARY 1999

Personnel

But there was more. Through the grapevine I came across officials who knew very well what was going on. DG XII, the DG for scientific research where I used to work, turned out to be a real hive of intrigue. Through Mrs Cresson's cabinet all kinds of staff transfers were arranged in the DG between senior officials. The cabinet insisted on French as the medium of communication and made sure that a lot of French staff were brought into the DG. With the cabinet's backing people made rapid progress up the career ladder even when they did not have the right qualifications.

Alfonso Torturi, a senior official with an impressive work record, had a reputation of being a bit of a Robin Hood. He was adroitly walked a tightrope between irregularities and honest dealings. He had close links with the Socialists and the Security Office and it was even rumoured that he had been involved as a middleman in the Agusta case, in which Agusta had paid bribes to the Flemish and Walloon Socialist parties.

Torturi wielded a lot of power. I saw that for myself one day during in the 1991 strike when he managed something that I, as a strike picket, had not been able to achieve. I looked on in amazement as all the strike-breakers on our floor were firmly sent away, even officials much more senior than he was. At the time all kinds of stories were going round about him. Apparently the doormen from the security firm were supposed to let him know if his superiors were entering or leaving the building. Much later I read in the file on the Security Office that he was in fact very well in with the security firm and was involved in a network that provided jobs for friends of local politicians through the security firm.

DG XII and DG XIII had a special staff budget for research and they were allowed a great deal of discretion to appoint any-one they liked without consulting the personnel DG. It was well known in personnel that influence was often brought to bear when people were selected for these contracts.

I was now busy looking for more information and bit by bit I discovered the following from various sources and statements.

When his contract was signed Berthelot turned up with Cresson and was unable to produce any written qualifications. In the end personnel settled for a brief CV provided by Cresson's cabinet.

There were three grades of 'scientific adviser'. In view of his age and recent career Berthelot appeared to qualify for the

higher grade (if he was an expert in the field), but Torturi insisted that Berthelot should be put in the lowest category (on about
£1,700 a month). He thought that DG XII was already being
charitable enough in doing anything for Berthelot at all. So for
Berthelot's first contract Torturi put him in the lowest category.
When the first contract was signed it was not known that
Berthelot also had a pension from his job in France. When that
was discovered later, personnel wrote a letter reclaiming the
money and the sum was actually offset against the follow-up
contract.

There was a problem with the follow-up contract because
after the pension had been deducted and the sum under the first
contract repaid there would not be much left over every month.
Berthelot complained about how little he had left. In the meantime Torturi was replaced by Nonscritta, who was much more
amenable to cooperation with the Cresson cabinet. Under pressure from Mrs Cresson's chef de cabinet, Bonmarché, ways were
sought to pay Berthelot more money. At an evening meeting in
Cresson's cabinet it was decided after some thought that in
future Berthelot would be paid a lucrative travel allowance,
which would be retroactive. This bore very little relation to his
actual travel expenses, since he often travelled in Cresson's car. So
these were official trips that Berthelot claimed to have to make
with Mrs Cresson. In the list of Berthelot's official trips that I saw
they were mainly trips to Chatellerault, where Cresson and
Berthelot lived. For these trips he claimed around £4,400 in
travel expenses.

In any event claiming travel expenses retroactively was irregular. One senior official in DG XII was reported to be unhappy
about this arrangement and was reluctant to sign the retroactive
claims, although eventually he did sign them.

It was also decided at two private meetings in Cresson's

cabinet that Berthelot should be put in a higher category as a scientific adviser. Financial Control had indicated that it had no objections; it was up to DG XII to decide how scientific advisers should be classified.

Eventually Berthelot was also given a contract through the Joint Research Centre from February 1997 to January 1998, for which he was paid in the region of £4,300 a month.

Altogether Berthelot must have received over £125,000 from European funds, broken down as follows:

1. Through Kensington Feb. 95 to Sept. 95 at £2,500 per month: £17,500
2. Scientific adviser (low grade) at £1,765 per month: £21,100
3. Deduction for French pension (estimate): £4,600
4. Payment for flat at £1,400 per month: £16,800
5. Travel expenses: £4,300
6. Scientific adviser (higher grade) at £2,300 per month: £27,300
7. Scientific adviser (Joint Research Centre) at £4,300 per month: £47,300

Torturi's promotion was held up by a dispute with the Cresson cabinet. The cabinet had brought Nonscritta in to replace Torturi in DG XII. From what I was told Nonscritta was not nearly as shrewd as Torturi. Under Nonscritta serious mistakes were made; for instance Berthelot and Cresson were shown in the Commission's address list as living at the same address. Apparently he was even foolish enough to fix his girlfriends up with jobs in his own department.

One DG XII official who was apparently doing his job too well was removed from his post and more or less suspended. For a year he wrote letters asking for his situation to be put right. The head of personnel attempted to keep him quiet with a favourable report. They even tried to give him another job, retroactively on paper for two years. Finally the official called for disciplinary proceedings to be taken against several senior officials for forgery. This case has still not been resolved and legal proceedings are in preparation against the management of DG XII.

A Wasted Journey?

One morning I stood at a station for an hour waiting for someone who was supposed to be bringing me papers on the Berthelot case. He had already phoned a couple of times putting it off and it seemed he was not coming that day after all.

Whilst I was waiting a homeless man came and sat next to me. He saw me reading the Bible and expressed surprise that there were still people who read the Bible openly.

I asked him how he ended up in his present situation. He replied that it was a long story. He was unlucky enough to live in a part of Brussels that did not provide any support for homeless people, although he used to get social security benefits. I asked if I could give him something and he was happy to accept. I said 'God bless you' and gave him a few pounds. He started explaining to me exactly what he could get to eat for that.

He asked me what I did for a living and I told him I was an EU official and had been suspended. To my amazement he had heard of me. He was better informed that some of my colleagues!

After a while a track worker came along and joined in the conversation. Eventually I left. I hadn't got the papers I was waiting for, but I had had an enjoyable conversation.

Later I spoke to my contact again on the phone. After talking about it with a few confidantes he had decided not to pass on the documents after all.

In any case I knew that the Committee of Wise Men already had various documents. They had asked DG XII to send them the Berthelot file. It had been sent, but certain documents had been left out, and that were really what the whole thing was all about.

All this happened in the few days before the Commission resigned.

After the Commission resigned

At the end of April I had just come back to work after my suspension. At lunch in the DG XII canteen I heard rumours about the Berthelot case, which I knew nothing about at the time. The Committee of Wise Men had apparently received not only incomplete files but also falsified documents, including some that had been backdated. A lot of DG XII officials who knew about this could not understand why it had not yet come out and in fact they were sitting waiting for the bomb to go off.

In May I had a visit from an official in the Security Office. I was hoping he would have something to tell me, but he just had to clear something up with me. It was to do with where Mrs Cresson's private address came from. I was supposed to have made it public. I asked him what made him say that and he showed me a Commission computer print-out showing an address I had given to an MEP, the same MEP who had attacked Mrs Cresson in February. It was just splitting hairs; anyone could easily have got hold of the address. I saw that the security officer had the MEP's file with him, but it was definitely thinner than the file I had seen.

I remarked that I thought there was something missing from the file. 'I'm afraid I can't tell you anything about that', the man said. I could understand that; after all he was only doing his job. Then I had a flash of inspiration and decided to ask him about the Berthelot reports. Again the security officer was reluctant to say anything, but I could see he didn't know what I was talking about. I asked him to wait a minute and came back with one of the 'scientific' reports by Berthelot, the 'AIDS expert'.

'I don't know anything about these documents', he said. He looked at them and then gave them back, saying, 'But I don't understand why you're showing them to me, they are not part of the investigation'. I explained to him that they were in fact relevant because the reports had been in the same file as the document incriminating me. I told him that the reports in the MEP's file came from my director general, Mrs Speculanti and not from me.

'Can you prove that?' he said. I nodded vigorously. 'I certainly can. Just look here in the top right hand corner. These are serial numbers that a member of the MEP's staff wrote on them. The serial numbers should also be on the other documents you have'. He looked in his file and had to admit that that was true.

I explained to him that Berthelot was producing these reports to try and prove he had actually done some work, but there were rumours that they were falsified or backdated. I emphasised that this was not favouritism but forgery. Did he want copies of all the reports? If so I might be able to get hold of them. He said he did. I later heard that the investigation about which the man had come to see me in the first place had been started at Mrs Cresson's instigation. Santer's cabinet must have been involved too, because they were responsible for the Security Office.

About a week later the security officer rang me up.

'Well, Mr van Buitenen, I have looked at them carefully and I wanted to let you know that your suspicions are correct. The documents are forged. You should inform OLAF (the successor to UCLAF), Mr van Buitenen, and send them a copy. You have a statutory duty to do that under the new rules'.

I did so, expecting the information to be new to OLAF.

Off the Record

However it turned out that OLAF already had the documents. DG XX had sent the whole file to UCLAF in August 1998. The French head of unit in UCLAF who was dealing with the file did find indications of irregularities at the time, but according to him there was no question of fraud. As usual UCLAF did not state this in writing. It was so much easier to do it verbally.

I found this out from one of my sources in Financial Control, who told me that my colleague Arnd Hannssen had already raised questions in 1997 about Berthelot's appointment for work for which he was totally unqualified. My informant confirmed the story that Mrs Speculanti had backed off. Apparently someone acting for Mrs Cresson had asked her not to reclaim the money. It was assumed that if the recovery letter was not sent the rumours would die down. That seemed to me to be pretty serious and I asked if there was any proof. But I could not get hold of any documents so I didn't know for certain who was involved. After the Committee of Wise Men recommended in their report that the money should be claimed back from Berthelot, Mrs Speculanti consulted the Commission's legal service about the possibility of recovering it. The legal service's advice was astounding: since the Wise Men's report had no legal basis, there was no new legal basis for reclaiming the money!

My source appeared to be well-informed about the case. For instance he was able to tell me that soon after she was appointed Mrs Cresson had given specific orders that Mr Berthelot was to be found a paid job in Brussels as quickly as possible. She had done the same thing in Paris when she was Prime Minister.

Mr Berthelot could not be given a contract as an expert or temporary official because he had already reached pensionable age. That was why they resorted to the 'scientific adviser' arrangement.

Later on I heard that Mrs Cresson had even threatened to the European Parliament that she would report other 'scientific advisers' who were not qualified. There were MEPs doing the same thing. According to my informant this arrangement was a well-known way of arranging jobs for friends. She said that almost half the 'scientific advisers' would have to be thrown out if they had to meet the high standards that would normally be required.

When I called to see Mr Desmond at OLAF I told him he already had the documents. I pointed out that the reports had probably been falsified. 'Maybe you should look into that more closely'.

OLAF in Action?

Desmond remained with one big question: had Berthelot written the reports himself, in which case the Commission had accepted forged documents, or had someone in the Commission written them for him? This was even worse because it meant that someone in the Commission had forged them. In that case OLAF would really have something to do.

In the middle of June someone passed documents on to me which I was very curious about. Things were getting crazier and crazier. Not only did the documents appear to be forged, but Mr Berthelot's claims for official trips had probably been made up later and signed by a senior DG XII official.

My informant could not say who had written the reports, but it was certainly not Berthelot. Judging by their amateurishness we guessed that it was someone in Cresson's cabinet. We felt that a scientific specialist in the DG would have produced something better. Some of the statistics came from a report by a senior DG XII official who was a personal friend of Mrs Cresson's chef de cabinet. But, my informant added, anyone could have copied the statistics.

I rang Mr Desmond in OLAF again and told him I had some new information. He was obviously interested and asked me to bring the documents in. I was curious to see how he would react to the file.

On the way to OLAF I fantasised about how it would be to work there. They really should have just taken me on, assuming of course that they now realised that I was right and that they wanted me. I thought about this and for a moment forgot all the problems with my job and the way I was being treated. I would at last be able to do proper investigations and not mess about any more. No more tedious accountants' investigations where it is more important to go along with the system than to get a result. I saw myself going through the Commission like a knife through butter. Who knows ....

In my heart I didn't really believe that anything would come of it, but even so I would have loved to work there.

In the report to OLAF I had tried to conceal my informants' identities as best I could. It was quite likely that they would focus on that point again. Instead of looking for ways of sorting the problem out they would be thinking about where I got my information from and who I had spoken to.

Desmond was waiting for me. He was obviously very curious. I explained the documents—over 100 pages of evidence—and left, saying, 'I hope you will actually do something with them'. He was somewhat amused at my mistrust, but I had good reason to be suspicious. After all UCLAF, OLAF's predecessor, had just looked at the case once and then put it aside as irrelevant.

I therefore decided after going to OLAF to ring the Court of Auditors straightaway and tell them what was happening. I phoned the chef de cabinet of a member of the Court of Auditors. We arranged that I would bring the stuff in a week's time.

Ten minutes later the phone rang. It was the Court of Auditors again. The member responsible had decided he should have the papers as quickly as possible. A driver came the following day and picked them up. I wrote an accompanying letter saying that OLAF was now dealing with the cases as well.

Lastly I made sure that the Committee of Wise Men were aware of the latest developments.

At the end of August some of the cases were leaked to the press. *The Sunday Times* reported on the cases in detail:

> *The disgraced European Union commissioner, Edith Cresson, presented forged documents to the European parliament when she defended herself against corruption allegations, according to an investigation by EU auditors. Cresson, a former French socialist prime minister, was condemned for spending £100,000 of public money employing her dentist friend, René Berthelot, as a scientific adviser. She may face police questioning over the origin of the documents which are believed by the auditors to be crude fakes. There is no evidence to suggest Cresson knew the documents were fake, but investigators hope she will tell the police exactly where they originated.*
>
> *The allegation threatens to cast a shadow over hearings before the European parliament this week to confirm the appointment of a new commission led by Romano Prodi, the former Italian premier. The previous commission, serving in an acting capacity, resigned in March over a fraud scandal that began with a furore over the hiring of the dentist.*
>
> *Yesterday Edward McMillan-Scott, leader of the British Conservative group, said the case was dynamite. 'The suspicion over these documents throws immense doubts on whether the public and MEPs have been told the truth about this corruption scandal. If proven, it would confirm our views of a culture of cover-up'.*
>
> *The 'Cresson papers'—each ostensibly a signed report by Berthelot*

addressed 'for the attention of Madame Edith Cresson' - are the subject of three official inquiries. A preliminary investigation by the Court of Auditors, the EU's financial watchdog, concluded that the documents are fakes and were typed up last year at the height of the controversy.

The EU's anti-fraud unit, OLAF, will hand a file to the Belgian police next month. A second report due out in the next fortnight by the so-called 'wise men', a committee of independent experts appointed to investigate EU fraud and mismanagement, is expected to reveal more details. It was this committee's last report, published on March 15, that forced the entire commission to resign. The employment of Berthelot, a friend of Cresson from her home town of Chatellerault, was described by the experts as 'a clear-cut case of favouritism'.

Arriving with Cresson in Brussels in 1995, Berthelot stayed at her home when in the city and was even rumoured to be providing 'astrological advice'. Speaking to The Sunday Times last year, Berthelot described himself as a long-time 'collaborator' of Cresson's.

'People are always trying to find a label for a person. Since I have a close relationship with Madame Cresson, they ask themselves: what is that all about? He's not her lover, so what is he?'

When Cresson, who remains acting education and research commissioner until the end of September, was asked last year to justify the employment of Berthelot as her scientific adviser between 1995 and 1997, she said the accusations against her were a 'German-inspired plot to damage France'. She added: 'As a politician, it seemed absolutely legitimate to call on external advisers, some of whom I know well'. Cresson then showed journalists and MEPs 10 reports signed and dated by Berthelot, aiming to show that he had done genuine work for the £100,000 he earned. But, each report was marked with the automatically generated code 'D(98)' which shows it was typed on a European commission typewriter in Brussels in 1998, not when Berthelot was employed.

The identifying marks, which show they were not genuine, had been left on, said a senior investigator.

If police were to question Cresson and her staff, it would require a decision by the commission to lift their personal immunity from prosecution. No commissioner has ever had immunity lifted.

… Cresson did not respond yesterday to messages left with her staff asking her to comment on the allegations.

SUNDAY TIMES, 29 AUGUST 1999

When I read that article I was delighted. It seemed my information was being taken seriously. But the most significant development was yet to come. The irregularities themselves were not so important. More to the point was how the departments and senior officials responsible (there were quite a few involved) had actually handled them.. Even now some curious decisions were being taken. For instance I discovered that at OLAF the file on Berthelot and Commissioner Cresson had been handed back to the same senior French official who had been unable to find any indications of fraud earlier! So I am interested to know when the full story will come out.

CHAPTER TWELVE

Paying the Price

The whole experience affected me and my family very deeply. Apart from the official opposition from my superiors, by 1998 I was starting to face all kinds of other problems, the most humiliating and unjust of which as far as I was concerned was being suspended in December and put on half pay.

Apart from the antagonism and disciplinary action I have described in previous chapters, there were other things happening and I did not know who was behind them. The most annoying part of these mysterious incidents was that it was easy to become too suspicious and people might, as a result, be less inclined to believe what I told them. So I tried to take the incidents in my stride and not let them affect me.

In October 1998 for instance my phone unaccountably stopped working for a day. I checked the lines of colleagues near me on the same floor and asked colleagues on the floor above if they were having the same problem, but it was only my line that was affected. The network connection of my PC was also not working that day, whereas my colleagues had no problems.

I rang the telephone service and the computer help desk, but they could offer no explanation. I was told the two problems could not be related because the systems were entirely separate.

When everything started working normally again the

following day I noticed that my PC was connected to a different wall socket.

'I can't understand it, wasn't it in a different socket before?'

The person on the help desk said, 'Not at all, Mr van Buitenen, you must have made a mistake'.

I knew for a fact that I hadn't made a mistake, because when the wire was plugged into the other socket I had sometimes tripped over it. After that I was much more careful when I used the internal phone line and the network. Someone might have been getting the equipment ready to tap and—without wanting to be too suspicious—I had to protect my sources. I usually made confidential calls on my mobile and I bought a laptop at my own expense to be able to work off-line.

At the beginning of November 1998 I had a call from the Commission's internal Security Office, wanting me to come for an interview. When I asked what it was about I was merely told cryptically, 'It's about the letter you wrote'.

I asked what the letter referred to but the caller refused to tell me, saying that the internal telephone lines were not secure. That was a remarkable statement, seeing that it is the Security Office itself that has internal lines tapped.

I refused to cooperate in an interview and asked the Security Office to contact my management. I told my director-general and head of department that I was only willing to be interviewed by the Security Office if they agreed and if I could be properly informed of my rights and obligations in the interview. I also wanted to know what powers the Security Office had and I wanted to be allowed to take my lawyer with me if I was interviewed.

In the meantime colleagues had told me what the interview was about. They had been interviewed too and it was about the anonymous letter to the European Parliament. Apparently I was regarded as the chief suspect.

Going Underground

There was another strange episode in December, when one weekend I had to flee from my home with all my papers. It was not my idea, in fact I was very reluctant, but I came under a lot of pressure. Various people - journalists and colleagues - rang me that weekend to warn me not to stay at home with the files. They drew my attention to reports of assaults and threats in the German and Belgian papers. One night the editor-in-chief of the daily *La Meuse*, which regularly published revelations and was highly critical of the frauds in the Commission, was attacked and assaulted. The ARD/WDR office in Brussels, which had a lot of files on Commission fraud, had a break-in. A contractor who had spoken out had a lorry driven over his Alfa Romeo. It was not clear whether the incidents were connected with what was happening in the Commission, but even so …

The final call that Sunday evening persuaded me. In fact a 'safe house' had been arranged for me. Besides other precautions, the files were divided between several cars. It was dark when we left. As we drove there I was just praying everything would be all right. All kinds of things were going through my head. When we got to the other house I was helped to carry all the bags and baskets of files and papers upstairs. Later, when I was on my own, I couldn't stop myself looking outside and checking the locks. Of course it had been a terrible experience for Edith and I gave her several rings on my mobile to say that I was well underway with all the files and later that I had arrived OK. Possible eavesdroppers would know that they need not bother trying to get into our house. Eventually, after midnight, I fell into an uneasy sleep.

Edith: 'After he got the call on his mobile Paul told me he was being advised to go away with the documents. Paul spoke on the phone to a couple of friends nearby and they thought the whole thing was clearly exaggerated. But we had begun to realise that such things don't happen only in films and it was best not to take any chances. A friend insisted that for our safety and his own Paul should get out of the house with all his material. He came to pick Paul up and take him away; he did not underestimate the risks and thought Paul should leave as quickly as possible.

There was something very strange going on. I realised how the situation might look to outsiders. They would think we were paranoid. Surely a government organisation wouldn't do anything wrong? If you couldn't trust a government organisation, what could you put your faith in?

So I stayed indoors with all the doors locked, the front door light on and the bedroom door wide open so I could see the stairs. I had not told the children the whole story. I wanted them to have a good night's sleep. Luckily Paul rang me while he was on his way and when he arrived to let me know everything was OK. That was a load off my mind. Where was it all going to end? I was really frightened'.

No Access

In December I found out that I could no longer log into the same networks and databases as my other colleagues in the Internal Audit. I went and asked colleagues whether they were having the same problem. They weren't.

I rang the help desk and was told my access was being restricted, but they did not know why. I would have to speak to their head of department. I was told he was not there. I could only get his secretary. I found it quite amusing though, because the part of the computer system they had screened off was virtually the only one I didn't need to get at my information. I had never accessed colleagues' personal databases without their express permission.

Post

After my suspension and also later, when I was back at work again in the buildings department, all the official letters from the Commission (of which there were quite a number) were sent to my home. I usually had to sign for them. They were formal letters, mostly about my position, my attendance at work and the whole business of my unauthorised sick leave. Sometimes the way the letters were delivered was fairly unpleasant.

Edith: 'It was early afternoon. Paul had gone to see his lawyer. A big dark-coloured Ford Scorpio with antennae on the roof and with European number plates stopped. It parked diagonally across our parking space in the front garden. Normally there was room for three cars there, but this car took up the whole space. The men in the car didn't look as if they had come for a friendly visit. A hulking great man with cropped hair and a long raincoat got out, while the other one stayed in the car. I waited for the door bell to ring and went to open the door, feeling a little nervous. What now?

The man simply said he was there on behalf of the Commission. Was Paul in? He wasn't. In that case could I sign for a letter?

I refused. I spoke firmly, although underneath I was really quite scared. I was wondering who this man was who looked like a bodyguard. Had he been specially chosen as the Commission's postman because of his build and intimidating appearance? The man shrugged and said in that case they would wait for Paul. He walked back to the car and the two of them sat waiting there, right outside the window. I went and sat in the kitchen so that I wouldn't have to see them.

I hoped Paul would be home soon.

In the meantime the press were beginning to gather outside the house again. The journalists had appointments with Paul and were waiting politely outside because they could see his car wasn't there yet. They had to park half in the street and outside neighbours' houses because the Commission car was in such an anti-social position it left no room for anyone else.

Later Paul told me a journalist from the French language press had rung him on his mobile to ask what was going on at our house. Were we under surveillance, because there were two funny looking men sitting in a big car with European plates which had been parked outside our house for quite a while? When Paul told him he knew nothing about it the journalist immediately reassured him. If anything happened, he would be there with his camera!

Paul came rushing home, worried about me and wondering what the Commission was trying to do to him now. So much trouble and intimidation to get a signature for a letter could only mean that the Commission was displeased about Monsieur van Buitenen's sense of duty'.

Isolation

Experiences like this and my suspension left me partly isolated. Only partly, because the people who approved of my action were wholehearted in their support. Those who disagreed with what I had done, on the other hand, showed it by avoiding me or not talking to me any more. Others were honest enough to say straight out what they thought.

On one occasion, shortly before I was suspended, I met a colleague in the Financial Control building. She spoke about my going to the European Parliament. When she was at home in her own country at the weekend people had been saying to her that it looked as though no one in the Commission took fraud very seriously. That made her feel extremely uncomfortable and she blamed me for that.

In January I spoke to two officials from the Commission's biggest trade union. They criticised me for going public about the irregularities.

'We know about a lot more cases than you do, Paul, but we chose to raise the matter in-house, inside the Commission'. They talked about irregularities that they had reported to the commissioner responsible years ago but he did nothing about them. And yet they accepted that. They thought that if I couldn't put up with the institutional culture in the Commission I should leave.

On Balance

Looking back over the past year, I wonder what I started. My action might have done something to make the Commission more critical towards irregularities and the way they are dealt with. It might even in the end make the organisation more transparent. At any rate the 'van Buitenen case' has been a catalyst for initiatives that were already under way, such as stricter monitoring of fraud and the transformation of UCLAF into the more independent OLAF.

However OLAF has yet to prove that it is independent. UCLAF was passive and not very effective, but OLAF is not really a new organisation. It still has the same people working for it and is still part of the Commission. How could Parliament have agreed to that? Why was OLAF not simply attached to the European Court of Auditors as an independent directorate? In my view that would have solved most of the problems at a stroke. It would have ensured that OLAF was independent of the Council of Ministers, the Commission and Parliament and at the same time there would also be independent supervision.

From a personal point of view, though, the outcome has been disastrous. Because there are no rules for 'whistleblowers' like me, I was suspended for four months on half pay, removed from my real work and shunted off into a job I would never have wanted. The constant opposition that I have faced has made it impossible for me to carry on doing my job properly in the Commission.

I might be a hero to many people, but in the Commission I am vilified and my career is at an end.

The Old Boy Network

The hierarchical mentality in the Commission is also to blame for what happened to me. Doubtless the previous Commission found it hard to accept that it had been forced to resign partly because of the actions of a B grade official.

Obviously people in the Commission think they owe their loyalty mostly to colleagues on the same level as themselves. The commissioners in the previous Commission stuck together until the facts were brought out in the open and they really could not carry on any longer. In July 1999 a senior official was still trying to protest his innocence through the 'old boy network' in a confidential note to Santer's chef de cabinet:

Thank you for your note of 5 July enclosing a copy of Mr Van Buitenen's document entitled The Berthelot Case. As requested

I'd like to bring the following to the attention of President Santer.

As a general observation I note that the document does not essentially add any new information to the knowledge of a case whose facts have already been examined in detail by the Committee of Independent Experts in its first report.

Apart from that the document contains a series of repetitive and sometimes contradictory allegations based on anonymous testimonies, calling into question the behaviour of various Commission officials including myself. I must point out that it is alleged in the document that I was proposing to intervene against the recovery of debts in relation to Mr Berthelot. I firmly refute that allegation, which is not supported by any of the facts. In fact, as far as I have been able to establish the question of recovery was mentioned only once in my presence. The decision in the present case can only be taken by the authorising department and the Financial Controller. My sole intervention was to recommend that if such a decision were to be taken the commissioner concerned should be informed beforehand. The initiative to set the recovery proceedings in motion was temporarily deferred pending the outcome of the investigation by the Committee of Independent Experts. Recovery proceedings have since been instituted by the authorising department responsible.

I hope the above explanation will put the allegations against me in Mr van Buitenen's document in their proper context. In this respect I welcome Mr Liikanen's decision to involve OLAF in the case and agree with you that the investigation should be stepped up. I am confident that the investigation will make it possible to clarify the facts and provide all the people against whom Mr van Buitenen makes allegations with an opportunity to express their views.

The official sent a copy to the president of the Court of

Auditors, the Committee of Wise Men, Commissioner Liikanen and the director of OLAF.

Nothing new? The new information in my files is not new evidence but the fact that the existing evidence was not properly investigated, which some even claim was deliberate. That was what I had been trying to show all along. I was not blowing the whistle on the irregularities themselves; usually that had already been done or they had already been exposed in the press. I blew the whistle on the way these cases were hushed up, the fact that they were investigated inadequately or not at all and nothing was done about them. Not only was no one disciplined but no steps were taken to make sure that nothing like that happened again.

It seems that the Berthelot affair will now be written off as a routine case of favouritism, certainly if Berthelot pays back his fees. But there is much more at stake. This time the favouritism went to such lengths that documents were forged in the Commission.

It would have been impossible for the Committee of Wise Men to find out about this from the very limited information available to them. They had very little time at their disposal (barely a month) and were not allowed to interview people under oath. In those circumstances they could only look at existing cases and reports. Even then they were forced to rely on material handed over to them voluntarily. They had to give a considered opinion on that material, which they did. In my file I also revealed the role of all the departments and senior officials involved in this case in detail.

It is true that the file is based partly on anonymous testimonies. It will be clear from this book why officials prefer to remain anonymous. I might have wished that things were different, but I respect my colleagues' decision, knowing how vulnerable officials are if they speak out. So I deliberately made it difficult to identify my sources. My report also explains how investigators could obtain corroboration of the testimonies I quote. I examine and point out the contradictions myself in the letter. It is also true that some of the testimonies overlap.

Given the possibility of a further investigation, the letter to Santer is understandable. The official was exerting all his authority to protest his innocence and show me up in a bad light. At the same time he covered himself by saying 'as far as I have been able to establish'.

When he mentioned the ongoing recovery settlement he was obviously still trying to keep the Berthelot scandal quiet- and perhaps also his own part in it.

No Decision From the Director-General

In accordance with the regulations my present Director-General, Mr Jansen, is the only person who can take a decision in my disciplinary proceedings, as Mr Liikanen and Mr Kinnock constantly tell MEPs when they express concern about my position. The investigation has already been going on since 16 December last year. By comparison with disciplinary proceedings in corruption cases my case is very simple. Nearly nine months later the director-general has still refused to take a decision, even after appeals on my part and a written plea. In fact he tried to step up the disciplinary proceedings against me after the outgoing commissioner Edith Cresson had ordered an additional investigation into my activities.

Before the European Parliament hearings at the beginning of September the commissioners-designate had to be briefed by the departments concerned. The Parliament gave Neil Kinnock, who would be responsible for personnel and the reform of the Commission, a comprehensive list of questions. These included a question on my situation, about which the Parliament was extremely concerned. It was pointed out that the Commission had acted with great speed when it came to removing a "whistleblower" from his job after he had passed on information which the Commission had withheld from Parliament. However it had failed to act promptly against staff involved in fraud and mismanagement. Mr Kinnock was asked how he would ensure that prompt action was taken against staff involved in fraud and mismanagement and how he thought the Commission should deal with "whistleblowers" like me.

Jansen gave Mr Kinnock an official briefing for his answer to the question. He said that it needed to be pointed out that this was not just an isolated case where someone had been prevented by the department from disclosing the truth; there were several matters involved, all at various stages of investigation. The general conclusion was that it was not a simple case of whistle-blowing where an official who is prevented from revealing the truth eventually has no option but to go public. This was an official who had, for whatever reason, decided to send both facts and opinions relating to a variety of cases to the chairman of a parliamentary political group. There might sometimes be instances where a whistleblower acted and was to be praised for his efforts but sometimes officials take matters into their own hands and completely disregard the official rules on secrecy and discretion.

The director-general is suggesting here that I acted irresponsibly and went out on a limb. What Jansen apparently refuses to see, although it was made clear in the interviews in the disciplinary proceedings, is that it was in fact a single case (Leonardo) in which an official (me) was prevented from revealing the truth. In my work as an assistant auditor in the Internal Audit Division of Financial Control I was able to see that similar things were going on in other cases. Other officials were being prevented from exposing the facts and were afraid to speak out. I considered it

my duty to make the situation as clear as possible. Not to outsiders but to the Parliament and the Court of Auditors. I did send
my letter to the chairman of the Greens on 9 December, but I
asked for copies to be sent to representatives of all the other
political groups on the budgetary control committee and that
was done the same day. It would actually have been better if I had
sent the letter straight to the budgetary control committee so
that it did not look like a political move. However I did think
very carefully about what I was doing and I would probably have
been protected under the new British legislation. I had already
been trying to report the problem inside the Commission for
more than a year, I was not seeking any personal gain, the matter was undoubtedly in the public interest, I chose the right institutions to blow the whistle to and I acted in good faith. Under
the terms of the new British legislation I was, in short, a whistleblower.

Fortunately Parliament had already listened to other points of
view. The Committee of Wise Men in particular took a different
view of the matter. In its first report on 15 March the committee confirmed the necessity for my letter to Parliament. Some
committee members thanked me afterwards and said I had
already done half their work for them!

The real issue is that everything went wrong at senior level.
Large amounts of Community funds were wasted, misappropri-
ated and spent on unsuitable projects and the commissioners
were aware of this. No one took any effective action and the person who blew the whistle on this is now being pilloried.

Rules for Whistleblowers

In the United States the law protects whistleblowers. Britain has
also introduced legislation, the Public Interest Disclosure Act
1998, to which the British organisation Public Concern at Work

made a vital contribution. This legislation is not perfect, but it is a good step in the right direction. I have approached various political groups in the European Parliament about the possibility of drawing up whistleblowers' rules for European officials. In March this year a huge majority voted against the motion, although it was supported by the Greens and many members of other groups. I am hoping that a new proposal that is now being drawn up will be adopted.

I was contacted by Professor Robert Bell, an American doing research into whistleblowers who had been looking for whistleblowers in Europe but couldn't find any. 'For a long time I believed there were no real whistleblowers in Europe. But then there was you!'

Obviously blowing the whistle is not an attractive proposition. In Europe it is investigative journalists who mainly perform that role. After my experiences with the Commission nobody else there will be too eager to expose irregularities in the future. The whistleblower who was planning to follow in my footsteps has wisely thought better of it. I think that that's a shame, but knowing what I know now I cannot really blame him or her.

At the moment I am being consulted by MEPs and staff of the commissioners-designate. That is all I can say about that at this stage.

I have certainly paid a heavy price.

CHAPTER THIRTEEN

What Comes Next?

An End to Secrecy

Why did all this happen? What was the cause of it, if any cause can be identified? In fact there is one constant theme running through this book: a secretive management culture. This is something that does not exist only in the Commission; the culture of secrecy is found in other organisations as well. Indeed, secrecy in large government bodies is the rule rather than the exception. People have often said to me, 'Why are you getting so upset about it? It happens everywhere. It's nothing new'. To which my reply is, 'Is that any reason to let it continue?'

It is not a small local authority I work for; it is a European government. The Commission is the highest public authority in Europe. More than any other government body it has a duty to set an example and operate the highest possible standards. That is the basic principle and intention in creating European institutions.

Unfortunately the reality has until now been quite different. The disclosures in the press, the Wise Men's reports, the reports by the Court of Auditors and the low turnout in the European elections are evidence of the need for radical reform of the Commission. Apart from various obvious measures relating to fraud prevention, codes of conduct and reviews of the organisation and regulations, one rule needs to be done away with immediately and that is the rule that you keep everything in-house. This all-important unwritten law that has up to now held sway in the Commission needs to be replaced by a principle founded on maximum openness in the Commission and in the other institutions. It is my firm belief that if we strive for maximum openness many of the problems described in the book will be solved at a stroke. In a culture of natural openness where people can express themselves freely, better control of abuses, lobbying, appointment policy and so on will automatically follow.

Measures in the Commission

Something really has to change in the Commission's administration. Contrary to what many people believe, the Commission's resignation in March 1999 will not necessarily lead to changes. The personnel might be different but there is a danger the system will stay the same. The change has to be genuine.

Disciplinary Measures

Many of my colleagues are generally sceptical about the likelihood of disciplinary measures against senior officials. One of the Santer Commission's last actions was to absolve a director-general of responsibility in the ECHO case in internal disciplinary proceedings. As director at the time he would not be held responsible for the irregularities in his directorate. In the Commission this was widely regarded as a flagrant breach of the general concept of what is just and right. Even the Court of Auditors asked the Commission for an explanation. The decision was particularly curious in the light of international trends in the responsibility of senior managers and directors. The positions of ministers in the Netherlands are under threat because of their predecessors' failures of communication (over the El-Al plane that crashed on Bijlmermeer), which are having a knock-on effect on the next government. Directors of private limited companies have had to accept much greater personal liability for their firm's activities.

Other Measures

Apart from the need to clean up the administration, other measures are also required. The Staff Regulations, for instance, have not been changed since the Commission was set up and they need to be updated. They should include a proper code for whistleblowers, similar to those in Britain and the United States. The Commission also needs to draw up proposals which will give the European Parliament a genuine right to institute inquiries. Besides that the status of the fraud prevention office is still in need of improvement. Its present position within the Commission, with a supervisory board to ensure independence, is a temporary expedient. It would have been more sensible to make OLAF part of the European Court of Auditors, which is truly independent.

The Commission's Memory

It is not a good sign that five of the commissioners from the previous Commission are still in office. These five, Neil Kinnock, Erkki Liikanen, Franz Fischler, Mario Monti and effectively also Pascal Lamy have sometimes described themselves as 'the Commission's memory'. Their experience is supposed to ensure a certain measure of continuity. In my view this continuity from the old regime is the last thing we need. To make a genuinely fresh start a clean break with the past is vital.

These commissioners were after all equally responsible for the things their colleagues did or did not do which led to the fall of the Commission. Whatever some members of the previous

Commission might argue, in fact all the commissioners are partly to blame for what went wrong under the last Commission.
This is inherent in the special decision-making machinery that I
referred to earlier. As I said in the first chapter, commissioners are
not there to represent national interests. This machinery was
designed to protect individual commissioners as far as possible
against influence from Member States and their own country in
particular. All major decisions are discussed jointly and in considerable detail. First there is consultation and negotiation
between the different departments, then consultation between
the cabinets involved and finally discussion by all the commissioners. After that a joint decision is taken and the decisions are
signed by each commissioner. It is therefore difficult for all the
other commissioners not to be aware of serious ongoing malpractice in a commissioner's field of responsibility. The commissioners who have apparently been declared blameless still need to
be reminded that they failed to address the problem adequately
or in some cases at all. They might not be personally guilty of any
misconduct but it does mean that they have a joint responsibility for the culture which now has to be relegated to the past.

Every large government organisation has skeletons in the
cupboard. The Commission is certainly no exception. The skeletons always emerge sooner or later, especially when you are trying to put the past behind you and establish a new management
culture. In letting members of the old team back in you are taking a risk, the risk that one of them was involved with or responsible for one of the skeletons, and then what are you going to do
about it? Would those commissioners then have to resign? Will
there be another Commission crisis?

I shall give a few specific examples. Franz Fischler, the commissioner for agriculture, was responsible for half the for
Commission's budget. The new commissioner, Pascal Lamy, was

President Delors' right-hand man ('sherpa', in his words) for about ten years. Erkki Liikanen was responsible for budgets and personnel and often defended the Commission's position in Parliament in the previous cases. It is true that in that sense they are the Commission's memory.

It would have been better to start afresh with an entirely new team, but that has not happened.

Hearings

Since it has been decided that these five experienced commissioners will be allowed to be part of the new team, one can only hope that they will genuinely put the past behind them. At the moment that seems doubtful, judging by their answers at the European Parliament 'hearings'. They have still not grasped the extent to which things have changed, as the following examples show.

At the hearings Commissioner Liikanen argued that radical reform of the Commission was much too difficult; he had done his best for five years but it was impossible to do very much. The truth is that no serious effort was ever made to reform the system in order to make it more open and change the culture. Commissioner Liikanen is not to blame for that. The time was still not ripe for reform at that stage. I know from various sources that in his way Mr Liikanen did his best to make changes, instance in the way people were appointed. But now the time is ripe for real change. I hope Mr Liikanen will recognise that and that he will act as a genuinely new commissioner.

As vice-president with responsibility for reforms and personnel matters, Neil Kinnock has a very important role in the new Commission. In this capacity he is also the person who will be dealing with my case.

It seems from Mr Kinnock's written answers in mid–August

that he does not see any problem with whistleblowers. OLAF is there for any officials that have problems and he says that you can always go to your own managers, who are then obliged to pass the information on. That makes me feel like saying, 'Are you kidding, Mr Kinnock?' He does not apparently see any need for European regulations or at least regulations for the EU institutions similar to those introduced by the Labour Government itself in the United Kingdom on 2 July (the Public Disclosure Act 1998) as a first step. Admittedly it is not entirely his fault; the briefing he has been given by the department responsible is totally misleading. So I am hoping Mr Kinnock will rethink his position and introduce a new and fairer system.

Expectations

The Prodi Commission therefore has very high expectations to meet. Fortunately there are a few signs that President Prodi is thinking along the right lines.

He has decided that the commissioners will no longer be based in one central building as they were in the past. They will be decentralised to their departments straightaway, so that they will at least know what is happening there. This is a first step towards dismantling a power centre that was closed to outside scrutiny.

The traditional custom of assigning particular fields of policy to particular countries is to stop. Top officials will be forced to move on regularly and inefficient commissioners will be relieved of their posts. Commissioners' cabinets will no longer be allowed to do executive work for the DGs and they will be smaller and more international in their composition.

President Prodi is promising a radical overhaul of the Commission's structure. In his speeches prior to his appointment he has frequently said that a new era of change and reform is dawning in the Commission, with efficiency, transparency and responsibility as its watchwords.

Transparency will be an absolute priority. With that in mind Prodi had information published immediately on the Internet when questions were being raised in an investigation by the Italian authorities about a company he had set up (although he himself is not accused of any misconduct).

I realise that the real changes are still to come. As I finish this chapter (5 September 1999) the Prodi Commission has not yet been appointed, so the new Commission has not had the chance to actually change course. On that understanding it seems to me that Mr Prodi has made a good start in announcing the specific measures described above. I sincerely believe that the new Commission is a step in the right direction—how big a step, only time will tell. I hope that this book has given the citizens of Europe a clearer picture of the European Commission. It is in Europe's interests for the Commission to be better understood, monitored and evaluated and that cannot be done without transparency.

The Need to Reform

On 18 January 2000 Neil Kinnock published his consultative document. In the introduction to his reform plans Mr Kinnock mentions that reforms are necessary due to a lack of service mentality, the change of society and new challenges like the forthcoming enlargement of the European Union. Mr Kinnock seems to forget a much more important and pressing issue, which is not mentioned in the introduction to his plans. Reform is necessary because of a lack of transparency and a failing administration, where it is difficult to find anyone who has even the slightest sense of responsibility (quote from the Committee of independent experts).

Mr Kinnock states that many of the present practices, conventions and regulations in the Commission are obstacles to a proper working of the institution.

I think this is an incorrect representation of the situation. The real problem is how the Commission administration applied the internal regulations which were already in existence. In the areas of staff management, disciplinary procedures, service provision and follow-up of audit reports in particular, the Commission did not properly utilise the procedures and regulations that are already available to them to use.

This implies that the introduction of a new set of practices, conventions and regulations, however necessary this may seem, would not automatically solve the problems which led to the resignation of the previous Commission.

Mr Kinnock refers in his Reform plan to several earlier reports that would have "provided him with valuable guidance". The reports of the Committee of Independent Experts are referred to as just two of the many reports available that offer instructive material.

The other reports referred to, however, are all internal Commission reports. From these, the Williamson Report was still a valuable internal exercise, in the sense that the staff were also allowed to participate. The other internal Commission exercises referred to; DeCoDe ("designing the Commission of tomorrow"), Sound and Efficient Management (SEM) 2000 and MAP 2000, are not well written or researched and really amount to little more than political statements by the European Commission.

In my view (and that of many others) the two reports of the Committee of Independent Experts are the only independent reports available with a sufficiently critical approach combined with the necessary expertise. The present short term proposals by Kinnock should have been based exclusively on these two reports. Other issues should have been given more time to mature and become the subject of a subsequent document later in the year, thus also matching the progress of the Inter Governmental Conference (IGC) and leading to proposals for further structural reforms.

Consultation of Commission staff?

In his preface, Commissioner Kinnock says that his reform plans are being published for consultation with the Commission staff and the other EU institutions. He suggests that in compiling the

White Paper to be approved by the Commission College on March 1st, account will be taken of the responses made through those consultations.

I have to say I am rather sceptical, particularly with regard to consulting the Commission's staff. His plans were not sent to the various Commission Departments for consultation, although they are the very people who will be affected. There are a lot of comments which the departments doubtless would have made, and these would have fundamentally changed the character of the internal discussions.

There are many clear signals coming from within several Directorate-Generals (DGs) inside the Commission that the staff is not being given a real and meaningful opportunity to provide input on the consultative document. The deliverance of the input is organised hierarchically, following a "pyramid" management pattern, while the deadlines for the input to be delivered are too tight and the terminology of the Consultative paper does not allow quick and easy digestion on the part of the reader.

I have heard from colleagues in several DGs, that the staff meetings that have taken place at unit level have not been of much use. The meetings were announced at very short notice and the extensive reform documents were only available a few days in advance. At these meetings, the majority of the staff present, including even the hierarchy, admitted that they had not yet had a proper chance to read Kinnock's plans, on which they were supposed to be commenting.

The submission of comments through a traditional hierarchical system such as that in the Commission, even with a much more extended time scale, has nothing to do with real staff participation. The pyramidal pattern serves as a filter for unwelcome comments to be sidelined.

Moreover, in some glaring cases of management inadequacy,

not to say incoherence, the invitations to submit comments on the reform plans addressed to the staff, were signed by the very members of the Commission hierarchy who had been identified by the Committee of independent experts as having been involved in irregularities themselves. There is even one case where a Deputy Director-General, himself being involved in a file that is under investigation by OLAF and the judicial authorities, requested his staff to submit their comments on the Consultative document within 36 hours. You couldn't make it up. Fact is simply stranger than fiction.

Also the possibility of staff submitting comments directly by e-mail on the face of it seems a nice idea, but no impact of this kind of participation can be traced. There is no control or any evidence of follow-up of the submissions made directly though e-mail by Commission staff. Indeed, acknowledgements are sent but there is no evidence of the promised follow-up actually being carried out.

Therefore we may conclude that the organised consultation of the Commission staff can hardly be taken seriously and that the exercise possibly only serves as an alibi for the Commission to pretend that there is a democratic basis available within the organisation for the reform plans of Commissioner Kinnock.

The only real consultative input into the reform plans on behalf of the Commission staff therefore has to come from the Commission's staff unions. They are the only platforms in the organisation where the staff can submit unfiltered comments on the reform plans. The unions face the difficult task of convincing Commissioner Kinnock of the necessity of a real dialogue, before finalising his reform plans into a definitive Commission Reform White Paper. If the staff unions do not succeed in this attempt, the reform process will have been carried out over the heads of the staff. The current attempts by Mr Kinnock to diminish the role of the staff unions and to have their participation taken over by official organs such as institutionalised staff committees, not only reflect badly on Mr Kinnock's history in the British trade union movement but they demonstrate a contempt for democracy.

It is simply not true that the unions would oppose reforms. In fact it is the unions who have been pressing for reform. What they have not been pressing for is a window-dressing exercise by means of a shiny and sellable reform manual that seems to be taken out of a management school course and just introduces a new set of rules without addressing the real problem.

Mr Kinnock should not try to hide behind the staff unions. He stated in a press conference on 14 December last year that "he faces considerable resistance to his plans from powerful staff unions".

The unions are not so powerful but they certainly want to co-operate with reforms, but only with real reforms on the right subjects. We would do better to avoid such inaccuracies, which merely serve to further the risk of blurring the agenda.

Central Internal Audit Service (IAS)

The creation of a Central Internal Audit Service (IAS) was recommended by the Committee of Independent Experts. To understand the importance of this part of the reform, I have to repeat and explain a few key observations from the expert reports on the functioning of the Commission's Financial Control Service. Especially with regard to ex-ante and ex-post control, and the difference between internal control and internal audit, some clarification is useful. I feel I need to address this somewhat technical subject in detail, as it provides a good illustration of what is wrong in the Commission and what is currently going on back stage.

Ex-ante Control

Ex-ante control are the measures taken to verify the legality and regularity of expenditure before it is made. Proposals for expenditure are checked for conformity with the appropriate rules and procedures and validated by the DG for Financial Control. Approval for an operation must explicitly be given before it can take place. This procedure is known in Community jargon as the granting of a "visa".

The experts noted that most of the irregularities reported by them stemmed from decisions to which Financial Control gave its approval. Behind this fact lies a substantial question mark about the effectiveness, indeed usefulness, of ex-ante financial control as currently organised in the Commission. The Financial Control department processes half-a-million financial transactions each year. This volume of operations has already led to a system whereby proposals are only studied on a sample basis (10% in 1999), with the great majority of operations therefore receiving automatic approval.

On this basis, the supposed "quality guarantee" provided by the visa is a myth, and the sense in which authorising officers feel correspondingly relieved of responsibility for the financial regularity of the operation is unjustified in either fact or principle.

Ex-post Control

Ex-post control are the measures taken to verify the legality and regularity of expenditure after or during expenditure. This category of control, although mostly performed as on-the-spot checks can also take the form of internal audits, which may be of specific services, programmes, projects, etc., carried out by a specialised service within Financial Control. Their conclusions ultimately take the form of reports by the Commission's

Financial Controller (i.e. the Director-General of Financial Control).

Contrary to the sample based ex-ante control activities, this audit division of the Financial control has played a crucial role in uncovering many of the cases of fraud detected by the Commission. It was this Division that I worked for. The experts also concluded that the Director-General of Financial Control is responsible for the failure to finalise the reports prepared by the audit division upon which action could have been taken.

This problem arises as a common thread throughout the experts' report. It frequently occurred that irregularities were identified in the course of audits by Financial Control, and that these irregularities were so clear that the need for swift remedial action was readily apparent. The prime example of this phenomenon was the Leonardo case, where observations (subsequently proven to be accurate) in early drafts disappeared in final texts.

Separation of Audit and Control

Both functions, though different in nature, include verification of conformity with the financial rule-book of the European Union, the Financial Regulation. Both ex-ante and ex-post control are currently grouped under the responsibility of the Directorate-General for Financial Control.

Two related issues lie at the heart of Financial Control's audit problems. First, the independence of the Director-General of Financial Control (Mrs Speculanti) vis-à-vis the auditee is compromised by the mere fact that, at present, both the visa and audit functions are directly under her responsibility as Director-General of Financial Control. One branch of the DG therefore potentially audits the actions of the other. Second, and in the light of experience more importantly, the Director-General of

Financial Control does not enjoy a position of authority over other Commission Departments. This authority is needed to make her independence truly operational. In practice, the position of the DG Financial Control as just one DG among others, and the corresponding position of the Financial Controller as just one high-level nominee among others, compromises her ability to translate audit findings into management action.

The most telling confirmation of this problem comes in the observation that numerous "sensitive" reports drafted by the Internal Audit Division have been the subject of lengthy contradictory procedures, often with the effect, and, one suspects, the intention, of delaying the report—and any consequent action— by periods of several months. Leaving aside for the present the need to introduce concrete measures to reduce the time taken for contradictory procedures to a reasonable level, these discussions tend to take on the nature of a negotiation between fellow Director-Generals. In this process, the purpose of audit—the detection and rectification of irregularities, the identification of systemic weaknesses and proposal of corrective action—is not necessarily of primary importance, as it is potentially overshadowed by the wish of both parties to come out of the process looking as good as possible.

The existence of a procedure whereby all transactions must receive the explicit prior approval of a separate financial control service has been a major factor in relieving Commission managers of a sense of personal responsibility for the operations they authorise while at the same time doing little or nothing to prevent serious irregularities. Moreover, the combination of this function together with a (weak) internal audit function in a single DG gives rise to potential conflicts of interest on the part of the Financial Controller.

As a conclusion it must be said that two functions, ex-ante

control and ex-post audit, should be considered as entirely separate (even conflicting) activities which do not and should not belong in the same department.

Where to audit and where to control

A professional and independent Internal Audit Service should be established. The centralised pre-audit function in Financial Control should be dispensed with and internal control - as an integrated part of line-responsibility - decentralised to the DGs. One of the principal tasks of the proposed Internal Audit Service should be to audit the efficiency and effectiveness of these decentralised control systems.

The Internal Audit Service should act under the direct responsibility and authority of the President of the Commission, Mr Prodi, independently of any other Commission Department. It should above all be a diagnostic tool in the hands of the President, enabling Mr Prodi to identify structural and organisational weaknesses in the Commission. The work programme of the Internal Audit Service should ensure periodic coverage of all Commission activities. It should however leave headroom for additional ad hoc audit tasks to be carried out at the request of the President or as needs arise.

So far the only observations have come from the Committee of Independent Experts.

Kinnock's plans with the IAS.

What are the implications of the Reform plan presented by Commissioner Kinnock in the light of these observations and recommendations?

He proposes to introduce a new, independent and professional Internal Audit Service (IAS). This IAS would be progressively built up on the basis of the existing internal audit in the

Financial Control DG. All this is in line with the recommendations of the reports of Independent Experts.

However, in direct contradiction to this, the current Director-
General of Financial control, Mrs Speculanti, has completely dis-
banded the present Internal Audit unit. For me this seems a
determined effort to settle a score with my former colleagues in
the audit division, which has played such a crucial role in uncovering many of the cases of fraud, despite the fact that Mrs
Speculanti failed to release the finalised audit reports, thus pre-
venting necessary action.

In an earlier draft of the reform plans, it was clearly stated that
the staff to be recruited for the IAS should be exclusively pro-
fessionally qualified audit staff. This was watered down to a proposal that in addition other competent staff from anywhere in
the Commission could enter the Internal Audit Service. At this
moment in time, I am picking up several signals in the
Commission which seem to indicate that Mrs Speculanti is now
trying get on board the new IAS some "loyal" staff even if this
would mean that they are not sufficiently qualified or professional for auditing work.

Tasks

As indicated by the experts, the work programme of the IAS
should ensure periodic audit coverage of all Commission activities and should also include ad hoc audit tasks in problematic
areas. The current proposal, however, seems to focus mainly on a
review of the audit techniques applied by the envisaged decentralised audit services. Although decentralised auditing is of value
to the local DGs, this can never replace a central and independent audit service.

The Place of the IAS in the organisation

As suggested by the independent experts, the IAS should be

reporting directly to the President of the Commission. However, in the plans proposed by Mr Kinnock, the IAS is placed under his responsibility as Vice-President for Reform. Furthermore, I hear that even this limited independence of the IAS is already under discussion. In my opinion, there is no possible compromise and Mr Prodi has no other choice than to accept the direct responsibility for the new IAS himself.

Controversial Events?

The discussion and preparation of the reforms with the unions takes place in different working groups in each key area. These working groups are chaired by members of the Commission hierarchy who are supposed to be experts in the area which has been attributed to them. It is evident that these specialised reform working groups can not be chaired by members of the hierarchy who are at the root of the mal-administration of the Commission departments. Nevertheless, it has been rumoured that the Director-General of Financial Control, Mrs. Speculanti is set to chair a working group on audit and financial services.

In October 1999, the Press reported the disappearance of a small shipment of Plutonium under the charge of the Commission Research Establishment as a result of human error and weak communication and organisation. After having travelled unnoticed through Belgium and Luxembourg, the shipment popped up in the UK. It was said that new procedures would immediately be put in place to avoid a repetition of the incident that had happened one month previously. In 0reality, the present security risks were already identified during a previous internal audit in 1997. Recommendations were made that could have avoided present security problems. Mrs Speculanti refused to clear the report, despite the recommendations of her own staff.

Transparency

More than new regulations or codes of conduct, the principle of transparency will provide a safeguard against the existence of favouritism, fraud, corruption, manipulation, conflict of interest or any other irregularities.

In the reform proposed by Mr Kinnock, transparency seems to have an important place. The words "transparent" or "transparency" appear about 20 times in the main document alone. In reality, these words change nothing. As long as an Official Secrets Act remains embedded in the staff regulations and is not replaced by a general right to speak for every civil servant, the principle of transparency in the Commission will remain a dead duck.

The Secrets Act is based on the following two paragraphs in the staff regulations:

Articles 12§1: An official shall abstain from any action and, in particular, any public expression of opinion, which may reflect on his position.

Articles 17§1: An official shall exercise the greatest discretion with regard to all facts and information coming to his knowledge in the course of or in connection with the performance of his duties; he shall not in any manner whatsoever disclose to any unauthorised person any document or information not already made public. He shall continue to be bound by this obligation after leaving the service.

These articles word in a very extensive and old-fashioned way the obligation of every official to keep all information inside the institution secret. It is as if the European Commission were a military secret service. Where is there a semblance of public spirit or openness in these intentions? Such provisions in the staff regulations make whistleblowing virtually impossible.

The wish of the Commission to keep the dirty linen inside at all costs, inevitably had to lead to the fall of that same Commission.

Rules on Whistleblowing

Whistleblowing is not a crime. It ought to be thought of as an important part of a modern and open administrative culture. Open and transparent organisations have nothing to fear from a whistleblower. Whistleblowing is not a "necessary evil". It is a guarantee against the persistence of structurally endemic fraud and irregularities. It is an illusion to think that stricter regulations or a perfect audit policy can wipe out all major irregularities. In my own practice as assistant auditor in the Commission, but also before I worked in Brussels, I have observed on many occasions that major breakthroughs in ongoing investigations could only be achieved with the assistance of responsible whistleblowing.

The independent experts confirmed that the events leading up to the resignation of the former Commission demonstrated the value of officials whose conscience persuades them of the need to expose wrongdoings encountered in the course of their everyday duties. They also showed how the reaction of superiors failed to live up to their legitimate expectations. Instead of offering ethical guidance, the hierarchy put additional pressure upon me.

Kinnock's reform plans only repeat the obligation of staff to report internally on evidence of the existence of possible fraud, corruption or any other illegal activity detrimental to the interests of the EU as well as on evidence of serious breaches of professional duties. It is self-evident that persons complying with the above obligations must not suffer from their actions.

This paragraph just states an obligation to report internally on certain issues and therefore has nothing to do with whistleblow-ing. The reform plan also suggests the creation of a central (inter-nal) mediation service to offer further assistance and a contact point for cases that do not involve alleged fraud or action affect-ing the financial interests of the EU. Although such a service is indeed useful, this has nothing to do with whistleblowing either.

In this context, whistleblowing should be considered as exposing to an outside person or body a malpractice or cover-up in an EU institution. As this goes directly against current EU staff regulations (articles 12 and 17), the whistleblower will inevitably be disciplined. It is this problem that needs addressing. Mr Kinnock's draft reform plan does not deal with this problem in any meaningful way whatsoever. There is only one line in the reform plan that indicates that this problem still needs solving.

Action point 47, listed in the attachments, states:

Beyond the existing procedures, the definition of external report-ing channels and the protection of whistleblowers and suspected persons needs to be taken care of.

No further details are given.

A genuine whistleblower will never pursue personal gain. He will always act in good faith, address a matter of sufficient inter-est, first report internally and finally try to address himself to a proper person or body outside the organisation. Each case of potential whistleblowing will be different. The degree of urgency, importance, stress, intimidation and availability of prop-er bodies to consult will differ from case to case.

Therefore it is by definition completely irrelevant to try to determine beforehand definitive external reporting channels for whistleblowing. A whistleblowing charter should be capable of dealing with any whistleblowing situation, including where a whistleblower has gone directly to the press. Each case of alleged whistleblowing should be assessed on grounds of whether the whistleblower indeed acted in good faith, did not pursue personal gain, addressed a matter of sufficient interest, had already reported the issue internally and finally tried to address himself to a proper external person or body. The judgement on each of these criteria depends on the specific situation at hand.

Such a whistleblower charter is not envisaged by the draft reform plan but must be included if it is to have any meaningful effect on Commission procedures.

Disciplinary Board

At the moment, the Disciplinary Board, like a board set up to "investigate" complaints of maladministration at the Commission, is a completely internal Commission body, whose members are exclusively Commission staff. The decision making procedures of the Board have, in practice, followed divergent criteria. The results of its deliberations and the decisions coming from the Board have been of very different quality and vigilance. Often one gets the impression that the main purpose of the internal Disciplinary Board is to keep the dirty linen inside, instead of investigating the circumstances of fraud and corruption and if necessary punishing the guilty. Senior staff with sufficient political protection are often not subject to appropriate disciplinary procedures or are freed of any further suspicion.

Sometimes, astonishing details about the proceedings in the disciplinary investigations as well as the administrative enquiries come to the surface. One example is that of an official who, at a certain point during an interrogation, refused to continue speaking without first consulting his Godfather ("Parrain"). Further informal inquiries made by me, seemed to confirm the existence of a Masonic lodge of which this official, as well as several other very senior staff, appeared to be a member.

Another example is that of an official who appeared to be immune to the efforts of the administration to launch a disciplinary enquiry against him. This senior staff member had been a member of two successive Commissioners cabinets. I knew this person and heard about his case as other colleagues made inquiries in an effort to identify the kind of political protection he enjoyed that apparently made him immune from disciplinary proceedings.

On some occasions the Disciplinary Boards have been abused to provide cover for staff who were guilty of irregularities, or to prevent the case from being transferred outside to the judicial authorities. On the other side of the coin, the Board may have been used to silence whistleblowers.

With these observations in mind, the proposal to introduce an external expert into the Disciplinary Board appears to be a good idea. As already indicated, these boards have been the playgrounds for internal networks. It is as if there have been no steadfast criteria on which judgements could properly be made.

Mr Kinnock suggests an external legal expert in an advisory position. I would suggest that something a little more radical is called for. In my opinion the inclusion of an independent and external judge as a stable and objective president on the Disciplinary Board would certainly be a step in the right direction.

Career development

It is evident that in a modern staff policy, career development and promotion should not only be based on age and seniority, but should mainly be based on merit. However, having said that, it should immediately be noted that under present Commission staff policy merit is a principle that, at least in theory, should play a major role in career development. So far, however, the Commission has not found a solution for a proper and objective application of the merit criterion. The simple statement that the career development should be based on merit is therefore an empty statement that provides no solution to inefficient staff management.

Also the proposal to prolong the probation period from 6-9 months to 18 months may seem an appropriate measure to avoid unqualified staff from getting a fixed contract, but in reality it is just window-dressing. The present probation period of 9 months for A-grades and 6 months for the other grades already offers ample opportunity to dismiss unsuitable candidates. The real problem is that these opportunities are virtually never used. To repeat the words that were used when I asked about the evaluation procedure at the expiry of my probation period: "If you did not shoot down your Head of unit and rape his wife, there is nothing to worry about!".

Nomination of senior staff

In the Consultative document, it is stated that the Commission will give more weight to the criterion of management abilities in selection/appointment procedures for senior staff. It will introduce individual performance assessments and performance of managers at all levels, including A1 and A2 officials, will be systematically evaluated. Moreover, appointments to all management positions will at first be for a probationary period. Finally, the principle of reversibility will be introduced: managers not reaching the required standard would revert to a non-management position.

In contrast with these soothing statements, the Vice-President in charge of staff and reform, Commissioner Kinnock, did not give a good example of the application of his own new proposals. Certain high ranking staff who had done a perfectly good job were brutally side-tracked from one day to another without warning. Apparently they had lost the necessary political support. Other staff that have been clearly addressed by the report of the independent experts have been confirmed in their posts or even been promoted. Those who have disclosed irregularities in their departments were punished and transferred, and those who were at the root of the same irregularities are still in place. This was one of the observations made in a recent 10,000 copy flyer that was distributed throughout the Commission departments. There was no reaction from Commissioner Kinnock. Later in this chapter I will present a specific example.

Staff Participation.

The reform document speaks of eroded job satisfaction and lacking of responsibility. What does Mr. Kinnock propose to improve this? His plans speak of new regulations, stricter codes of conduct, calling in of external expertise, the obligation to follow training. He has also shown what he understands by consultation. It can surely not be Mr Kinnock's intention to solve the problem of job satisfaction and lack of responsibility with such an approach.

An omission in the proposed reform plans is a vision of how to bring back to the Commission staff the job satisfaction they need to work constructively, to think pro-actively and to have the guts to take responsibility for their actions. A solution that I would look for is a way to ensure real staff participation in the working processes. On the work floor the signals towards inefficiency, delays and irregularities can be picked up easily and dealt with before the system derails. The staff should have the possibility of influencing their working process and be encouraged to forward their comments on a regular basis without the risk of incurring negative repercussions. Direct feedback from their hierarchy should be automatic.

When I addressed my own management hierarchy with my comments on the way how they dealt with the follow up of audit reports, I was silenced and discharged from my obligation to inform my hierarchy further on the subject. This is the root of the problem, which is still not being addressed.

Another suggestion that could be raised relates to staff reporting processes. As part of merit evaluation, in Kinnock's plans the core of new career development, a procedure should be introduced whereby subordinates evaluate the performance of their hierarchy on a regular basis.

The Staff Regulations

As in many other areas, it is very important to note that many of the present problems, as presented in both reports of independent experts, are not due to deficient staff regulations, but due to a false application of the present staff regulations that already exist. It is a widespread myth that the present Commission staff regulations are over-protective. The problem here is that Commission hierarchy has not bothered to use the possibilities that exist under the present staff regulations to encourage a dynamic staff management, to reward more directly and to punish more efficiently. The existing staff regulations already offer opportunities to dismiss an official, to deny him his pension rights and even to recover from him any losses that the EU institutions incurred because of his professional behaviour.

Having said this, there are only a very limited number of articles in the staff regulations that urgently need updating.

The most pressing examples are articles 12 and 17. As already indicated, these articles obstruct the functioning of transparency in the European Institutions. Another example is article 21, which says that Commission staff should inform their hierarchy of existing problems. This article should be extended to introduce the obligation of the hierarchy to report back to their subordinates on what they have done with their reports and complaints and, if applicable, why no action was taken.

The Present Situation

So, as I write this at the end of the first month of the new Millennium, what is the situation like now? Has anything changed yet? With regret, I have to say that so far the answer seems to be 'No'.

The European Commission is still in a serious crisis. Although the conclusions of the reports of the Committee of Independent Experts, published on 15 March 1999 and 10 September 1999 were very clear and to the point, the new Commission has, so far, singularly failed to take the necessary steps to improve the situation. As a clear illustration I will give an update on the case of Mrs Cresson's dentist.

Even in Mr. René Berthelot's case, the simplest and clearest case, labelled in the first report of the Committee of Independent Experts as a clear-cut case of favouritism, the new Commission has not shown enough resolve to take the appropriate steps:

1. Early in 1995, the cabinet of Commissioner Cresson initiated a contract with Mr. Berthelot, not through a regular Commission contract or a contract in line with Belgian legislation, but through an offshore company. This company was part of the Perry-Lux network that received substantial financing of many Commission departments and proved to be involved in fraudulent contracts with the Commission. Has the new Commission committed itself

to taking the necessary follow-up actions?

2. Despite clear indications towards fraud, UCLAF concluded in 1998 that no further investigation was necessary. Are there any consequences?

3. Contrary to the recommendations in 1998 of the auditors in charge, and to the advice of the Deputy Financial Controller, the Director General of Financial Control did not suggest (neither to DG XII nor to JRC) issuing a recovery order.

4. The Independent Experts once again recommended a full recovery on 15 March 1999. At the request of Financial Control, the Legal Department examined the case and wrote in April 1999 that this alone did not constitute a sufficient legal basis to initiate a recovery. I could hardly believe my eyes.

5. After the file was resubmitted by me to OLAF, the Secretariat-General wrote on 6 July 1999 that no new element has been added to a file already largely investigated. The note even seems an effort to ridicule the request for re-examination.

6. On 1 September 1999 an inter-departmental meeting with five (!) (Deputy-)Director-Generals present, took place. Again, no action was decided upon. From the minutes of the meeting it is apparent that it was more like a 'cover-my-ass' session. These staff are still in charge of their respective departments.

7. On 11 October 1999, even the "Union Syndicale" (traditionally the biggest staff union in the Commission) wrote an open letter to Research Commissioner Busquin, with copies to all staff, claiming that no further action needed to be taken and that it was absurd to blame the hierarchy for merely having obeyed orders. Where have I heard that before?

8. On 25 November 1999, following a report of OLAF, the Commission confirmed publicly the opening of disciplinary procedures against five officials concerning this case and that the report was being sent by OLAF to the Belgian judicial authorities. The Commission did not bother to suspend these officials as "OLAF did not state that suspension was necessary" (sic) and no decision to move these officials to another post within the Commission has since been taken. Since when does OLAF also decide on disciplinary measures to be taken against staff?

One year after the first report of the Committee of Independent Experts, one year after the Commission's resignation and five months after the arrival of the new Commission, the citizens of the European Union are still waiting for the final results of all these notes, meetings and investigations undertaken in such an open and shut case. They still do not know if and when the Commission will recover the taxpayer's money paid to this contractor who failed to produce even a minimum quantity of work of interest to the Commission. Recovery from Mr Berthelot may be difficult, but there is also the possibility under the present staff regulations, to recover the money from the Commission staff in case of proven serious professional deficiency. Why does no one raise this possibility?

The DG Research hierarchy, which was responsible in the first place, is still in place. They have been confirmed on their tasks and no reform whatsoever of these departments has been undertaken by the new Commissioner, M. Busquin.

Is all this in line with the principles of "Accountability, Responsibility, Efficiency, Transparency" on which the new Commission wants to build its action and on which Mr. Kinnock's reform proposals are based?

One should keep in mind that Mr. René Berthelot's case is the simplest and clearest case mentioned in the first report of the Committee of Independent Experts. Has the devastating observation of the Independent Experts, made back in March 1999, still not been heeded?

> "The studies carried out by the Committee have too often revealed a growing reluctance among the members of the hierarchy to acknowledge their responsibility. It is becoming difficult to find anyone who has even the slightest sense of responsibility."

Mr Kinnock cannot be taken seriously in claiming that his reform plan is designed to achieve an organisation capable of exceeding the best standards (sic), if the real issues are not properly addressed.

It is still my sincere hope that the new Commission no longer continues to deny in practice the appropriateness of the Experts' conclusions and acknowledges the seriousness of the situation which still persists at a high level in the Commission departments.

If the new Commission still refuses to take appropriate action, I must assume that the will for a genuine reform of the Commission administration is sadly lacking.

Proposal for a Better Procedure

Political Context

A proper reform process has to be studied, prepared and implemented carefully. The present proposals do not seem to follow this path. The priorities are not set against short term and long term objectives and are being mixed up, while consultation with the Commission staff involved appears to be superficial at best. The reform plans of Mr Kinnock read like a management course manual and seem to have as their principal objective, the selling of the reform to the press and the public. It can not be denied that a well-spun reform would surely be a welcome present for the Prime Minister, when he has to deliver on his promise to hold a referendum on UK entry into the European Single Currency.

Immediate Measures

The problems that led to the resignation of the Commission, which were identified and confirmed clearly by the Committee of independent experts are well known. These problems have nothing to do with a changing society or forthcoming challenges such as the EU enlargement. Therefore, in order to address the immediate problems in the Commission, it suffices to initiate immediately a minimum number of requisite changes. These can be drawn directly from the reports of the experts. As no fundamental reorganisation is necessary for this, these changes should (and could) be carried through as soon as possible.

Commission staff are not resisting reforms, indeed they are asking for proper reforms. Staff participation is necessary to ensure that they are motivated again. In my opinion, the reform plan does not address the real problems. We should avoid plans that look good but risk solving nothing.

Longer Term Proposals

The changing role of the Commission and the forthcoming enlargement necessitate more radical and longer term reforms. Reforms are needed to ensure the biggest enlargement in EU history does not paralyse decision-making. The EU's institutions, created for six members, now have 15 and could in the next few years have 28 members. The member states will decide during the intergovernmental conference (IGC) whether to adopt bold reforms or opt for a minimalist approach of less far-reaching changes. The IGC starts on February 14. The changes must be agreed by December and completed before 2003, when the first of 13 new countries could become members. The shape of these reforms and the tasks to be entrusted to the Commission can only be identified if the new role of the Commission in the enlarged EU has been made clear. This should dictate the guidelines for longer term reform policy and not drive the Commission in a short term stir-up that does not benefit anyone but a few politicians.

A Final Word

We all know fraud exists in the EU-institutions, but that is not the issue. I want to point out that we can do more about it. Fraud on political level does not only exist in Brussels. Some people who sent me letters from the UK, think that in the UK the situation is much better. I would say that it has been shown recently that fraud exists everywhere, not only in Italy, France or Belgium, but also in countries like the Netherlands and Germany. I am afraid that the UK is no exception.

in brief, we could say that Europe's social dimension and way of decision making, not only within its own institutions, but also in the member states, needs serious attention. Some politicians seem to suggest that flexible fundraising and creative accounting should be possible if it is for a greater purpose. Is that so? Does our conscience whisper to us in the ears to create a bigger common market at all costs? I don't think so. But it does remind us of honesty and openness. Dirty linen should not be kept in dark places where it starts to putrefy. It will then affect the environment. Dirty linen should be washed in the open to keep Europe clean. The European collaboration is too important to be decided in closed networks. How or even if, European collaboration should go towards unification is a decision that should be prepared and decided in all openness.

With this book I hope to contribute to that part of the transparency that was missing.

You can find out more about the proposed reforms of the European Commission at the following internet addresses:

Paul van Buitenen
http://www.buitenen.com/

European Commission
http://europa.eu.int/comm/index_en.htm

Report on the reform of the European Commission
http://europa.eu.int/comm/reform/index_en.htm

Commissioners' Interests
http://europa.eu.int/comm/commissioners/interests/index_en.htm

Parliamentary Hearings of the Commissioners Designate
http://europa.eu.int/comm/hearings/index_en.htm